In Memory ... or,
Love, Papa H.

ALSO BY NICOLE SAPHIER, MD

Make America Healthy Again: How Bad Behavior and
Big Government Caused a Trillion-Dollar Crisis
Panic Attack: Playing Politics with Science in the
Fight Against Covid-19
That's What Family's For

Love, Mom

INSPIRING STORIES CELEBRATING MOTHERHOOD

NICOLE SAPHIER, MD

HarperCollins books may be purchased for educational, business, or sales promotional use. For information, please email the Special Markets Department at SPsales@harpercollins.com.

An extension of this copyright appears on page 227.

FIRST EDITION

Library of Congress Cataloging-in-Publication Data has been applied for.

ISBN 978-0-06-332565-4

24 25 26 27 28 LBC 5 4 3 2 1

For Nicholas, Hudson, and Harrison,
because without you, I wouldn't be me.

For my mom and the cadre of people
who helped me follow my dreams.

And for moms everywhere, you are God's angels.

"Motherhood:
All love begins and ends there."

—ROBERT BROWNING

CONTENTS

INTRODUCTION

"There's no way to be a perfect mother and a
million ways to be a good one."

—Jill Churchill

MOTHERS CARRY the awe-inspiring responsibility of raising generations of people.

As a mother myself, I know the joy of being a mom, as well as the
struggles, fears, and frustrations it can carry. I carry them, too.

There are so many hero moms who not only inspire me to be the
best mother and person I can be but also help me accept that being
perfect isn't possible. They remind me to forgive myself if I can't be
everything to everyone at all times.

The women in this book are heroes to me, because they do all the
unglamorous mom things we do for our kids—from wiping tears and
noses to cheering from the stands at Little League games, hanging
artwork on the refrigerator, car pools, laundry, watching our kids
make mistakes, and helping them learn from them and pick up the

pieces—and because they do it while juggling various other tasks and despite obstacles being thrown in their way.

From the everyday, small choices we face to the big, life-altering decisions, moms are entrusted with heavy responsibilities while also ensuring the wellness of their family. The pressure is monumental, but the reward is immeasurable.

Every mom has a story.

This is a collection of such stories from some of the most incredible moms I know. Some are colleagues and friends from FOX; some I found from my personal and professional interactions; and others are from some amazing FOX viewers. Each one of these moms shares part of her life with us in her own words. Ainsley Earhardt talks about leaning on her faith after divorce and realizing how precious the bond is between a mother and daughter after losing her own mom. Janice Dean shares the greatness of raising boys while also dealing with the devastation of miscarriage and living with an autoimmune disease. And Annette Hill, a Gold Star mom, talks about tragically losing her only son and continuing forward while keeping his memory alive. Every story is unique and shares powerful common threads: Resilience, Faith, Purpose, Valor, and Acceptance. As I listened to each woman tell her story, I discovered another connective theme: almost every mom in this book pointed to her own mother as a hero—and was excited to share words of wisdom that were passed down to her and helped mold the mother she became.

All of the moms in this book have incredible insights from their own journeys to pass along; their stories will make you cry and laugh, and hopefully, as you read, you will begin to accept that it is okay not to be perfect all the time. You are perfect to those who matter.

I hope you'll be as inspired as I was when I heard these stories that celebrate what it is to be a mom.

It's everything.

PART I

Resilience

We often take good health, both physical and mental, for granted. When we are faced with an unexpected illness or an obstacle that leads us to an uphill battle, it takes not only extraordinary physical resilience to fight the fatigue we are facing but enormous emotional resilience to combat those barriers playing out in our mind.

But we all have it in us to cope with more than we ever thought we could—and we are stronger than we give ourselves credit for being.

CHAPTER 1

Nicole Saphier, MD

Breast Radiologist, Memorial Sloan Kettering Cancer Center;
Medical Contributor, FOX News

"Two roads diverged in a wood, and I—
I took the one less traveled by,
And that has made all the difference."

—*Robert Frost*

Motherhood is an extraordinary journey that brings boundless joys and immeasurable fulfillment. Amid the joys, however, lie a unique set of challenges that demand unwavering resilience and determination. In the pursuit of our dreams, it's expected that we follow the well-trodden path that society lays out for us. However, sometimes things don't go as planned, forcing us to make a choice as we stare ahead at a crossroads. For me, that pivotal moment was when I became pregnant at seventeen. Over the almost three decades since then, I have learned that when we are faced with obstacles, it takes courage and conviction to veer away from the conventional routes and forge a new path that may be untested. By embracing the path less followed, we can not only overcome the most formidable challenges, but unlock our full potential, hopefully leaving an indelible mark on other people's lives.

From Point A to Point B

I had always assumed I would eventually be a mom. As I was growing up, my plan was to become a doctor, marry the man of my dreams, and have children. Pretty straightforward. In truth, that was what happened, but it wasn't in that order and hardly felt as if it were on my terms most of the time.

My parents were East Coast born, but both escaped out west for college, where they met, fell in love, and had me. That young love ended in divorce when I was only two, but I was always their priority and never felt unloved. I admit, I'd take advantage of the separation and if my mom said no to something I wanted, I'd just ask my dad and hope they wouldn't talk about it. I was a tomboy in my younger years, an athlete, an honor student; you really couldn't fit me into one category. Throughout my teen years, my faith grew strong. Though my dad was raised Catholic, my mom was Episcopalian. I found my own community at a Catholic church near our home and regularly attended teen Mass, Bible study, and Rosary on my own. It was a very important aspect of my life.

During my adolescence, competitive cheerleading and gymnastics consumed my time outside school, and because of that, by age sixteen I needed my first knee surgery to repair a torn ACL. My coaches were tough and told me I wouldn't be allowed back in the gym until I was able to train again. That gave me the motivation to prove that I was as good as anyone else despite my injury and pushed me to competing again before the doctors recommended. Because of my haste, my knee gave out and set me back months. Rather than practices and competitions, I was now in rehab daily without my friends, without my coaches. It felt as though a huge piece of me was gone. Unfortunately, it sent me into a downward spiral mentally.

My mom is a licensed clinical therapist and works with children with mental health issues in the thick of the worst, removing children from dangerous homes and helping trafficking victims. Although that's a far cry from the adolescent turmoil I was experiencing, she was always attuned to my needs and keenly aware that I was struggling with signs of depression.

She was concerned enough to ask my coach if I could participate in another role, such as coaching the younger kids, to help me out of the slump while I was in rehab. He said no, and I reacted like an emotional teen: I lost it. I threw away all my trophies, awards, and team photos in a fit of hysteria, leaving my bedroom walls bare and void of any personal touch.

I wasn't always nice to my mom during that turbulent time, but she was by my side. I frequently had bad dreams, and when I told her about them, she would interpret their meanings. Looking back now, it was such a nice moment between us and showed the incredible insight she had into my soul; at the time, I found it very annoying.

I can't remember the dreams specifically, but I do remember feeling as though there was something stuck in my throat during some of them, making me believe that my dream was telling me that there was something inside me that needed to come out. I wasn't the perfect child; I was doing some things at the time I shouldn't have been doing. I never did drugs, but with my days no longer consumed by practice and competitions, I tried alcohol and was not wholly truthful with my parents about my actions. My mom told me she believed that my dreams were the manifestation of shame I might be feeling due to keeping negative thoughts or behaviors inside. She was right.

I was seventeen. It was the summer between my junior and senior years of high school. I began feeling very tired, and I didn't have the same amount of energy I usually had. I attributed the change to being out of the gym. After realizing my period was late, I couldn't ignore my symptoms any longer. One morning, rather than driving to school, I bought a pregnancy test at the local pharmacy. Actually, I bought five. I didn't even leave the store; I took a test right there in the pharmacy restroom. Waiting the few minutes for the results was agonizing, and when it came up positive, I convinced myself that it was a false positive. So I took another one and another after that. After taking all five, I could no longer deny the reality.

I left the pharmacy in shock. Unable to process the information alone, I pulled my best friend, Mandy, whom I'd known since early childhood, out of school and told her. She was as stunned as I was. There was only one thing to do. Together we drove straight to my mom's work. I knew if I was facing something, whatever it might be, it would be better with my friend by my side, and I knew I needed to tell my mom. I had never been good at keeping secrets from her anyway.

I remember the moment vividly. As I walked into my mom's office, I was so nervous that I could barely breathe. She looked up from behind her desk, eyes wide, because this was obviously not normal; we should be in school, yet we were in her office. She knew something was wrong.

Mandy and I sat down in front of her, and I blurted out, "Mom, I'm pregnant."

She was quiet for a moment, then took a deep breath and said calmly, "Okay, well, there are lots of big decisions ahead, but just know that whatever you decide, I'll be right here by your side through it all."

I cried a bit as I gave her a big hug, and she squeezed me back, crying, too. That was everything to me, my mom just loving me and not showing her disappointment at the moment I needed her love the most.

I went back to school that day.

THE NEXT FEW weeks were pretty surreal. The hardest part for me was telling my boyfriend and then my dad; both had very different reactions from my mom. The gravity of the situation paralyzed them both. Neither was able to imagine a way that going through with the pregnancy would afford a good life. They both regret their initial reactions now, but at the time I was a scared seventeen-year-old and could have used more support. I don't know what I expected, but my boyfriend and I broke up, bringing the reality of being a single, pregnant teenager into sharp focus. It was overwhelming.

My mother was right: there were huge decisions to be made. My world had turned upside down overnight. Up until then, I had always gone straight from point A to point B in achieving my goals, constantly asking what my next step should be and planning how to get there: I'm going to this next level in gymnastics, I'm taking this next math class. I had things planned out. I had always wanted to be a doctor, knowing that after high school graduation the next step would be to go east, move to New York City for undergraduate school and then medical school. That had been the plan. Now I wasn't sure that any of it was possible. I was scared. I was sad. And I felt lost.

I kept thinking, "You're going to spend your senior year of high school pregnant. You're going to be a statistic, that pregnant teen walking the halls."

And I was—because after the initial shock, and worry about my future, I made the decision that despite the unknowns, I would have the child and there was no one who could change my mind. Believe me, many people tried. No matter how much it would change my life, I knew in my heart that a little being was growing inside me and it was my job to protect him.

I tried as long as I could to hide my pregnancy, but eventually it became obvious, and when it did, I realized that those I considered friends were anything but. Most of the people I'd hung out with for years, whether studying for the debate team, traveling the country for cheerleading competitions, or hanging out at the lake on weekends, rejected me. They would barely look at me when I passed them in the halls, let alone ask me how I was doing. A few even told me I'd be ruining my life, as well as my ex-boyfriend's life, and that I shouldn't go through with it. My teachers weren't much help; they didn't acknowledge me much, as though my mere presence made them uncomfortable.

It didn't help that after I began to start showing, I was gently asked not to attend the teen Mass and other youth programs at my church. It broke my heart to be cut off from the community that was so important to me. As a result, I stopped going to church altogether—and it would take a long time for me to go back. I didn't lose faith in God. In fact, I read my entire Teen Bible from front to

back during my pregnancy, drawing sources of inspiration and answers from many stories.

I tried to keep my chin up and press on. I didn't interact with
many people outside of my family and my coworkers at the YMCA.
I did what I had to do for school and work, then would quickly go
home.

A small cadre of friends rallied around me. Michelle, someone
whom I hadn't been close to previously, stepped in and became the
companion I desperately needed. I don't know what it was in her
heart that made her cling to me and show me so much love and support, but I'm forever grateful that she did. She would come over after
class to ask me about my day and make me cucumber and cheese
sandwiches, my pregnancy craving. She didn't have to, she just
wanted to. Not once did she make me feel ashamed of my situation
or appear embarrassed to be seen with me. It felt as though she loved
the baby inside me as much as I did. She still does. I can't thank her
enough for what she meant to me during that difficult time. She
was a huge part of the emotional support that kept me from slipping
into a lonely abyss.

Another person who kept me going was my friend Michael, a
gifted musician who played guitar and sang in coffee shops after
school and on weekends. Before the pregnancy and while I was recovering from my knee surgery, he would come over weekly to watch
Dawson's Creek. We used to laugh and wonder which of the characters we were most similar to. I was convinced that I was most like
Joey Potter, played by Katie Holmes—the feisty, loyal tomboy.

Even after I became pregnant, he didn't stop our ritual and continued to show up every week at my house.

One night after watching our show, Michael said something to
me that changed my entire mindset. I shared with him what other
people were saying to me: that I would not reach my dream of

becoming a doctor because of the pregnancy and that I was ruining my life. Some were suggesting that I take some time off after high school or go to college part-time while I figured everything out. I confided to him that I was worried that if I took time off, I wouldn't make it back on track to reach my goals. I'll never forget him taking a piece of paper and drawing two points on it without saying a word. Then he drew a straight line between them. He said, "This has been your path your whole life. Your line has been straighter than anyone I've ever met." Then he drew a semicircle connecting the two points. "You're still going to get from point A to point B. You're just taking a different path now. Don't worry, most of us take this curved path most of our lives. It will be a change for you, but you're still going to get there. That is who you are."

His words and visuals were enough to convince me that I could still be everything I wanted to be. He gave me a renewed sense of motivation to reach my goals and also to prove everyone who was saying I couldn't wrong. I spent the next couple of decades doing just that.

I still had anger, sadness, fear, and a lot of other emotions inside as I finished my senior year of high school. But my family and a few close friends who were giving me a safe space, loving me, and believing in me were my biggest sources of strength.

Not Your Typical College Experience

Nicholas was born in April 2000, and five weeks later, I walked across the stage at graduation to accept my high school diploma. My mom and dad held my newborn in the stands like Rafiki from *The Lion King* holding up baby Simba for the entire pride to see. It had not been the senior year I had planned; I hadn't gone to senior prom or done other things kids my age were doing. By graduation, I was breastfeeding, changing diapers, and getting to know the incredible new little person in my life. It was scary at times, but I never doubted the decision I had made to have him. His beautiful blue eyes looking up at me were all I needed to give me peace.

I had come to grips with the reality that as a single mom, it wasn't in the cards for me to go to college in New York City, three thousand miles away from family and friends. But I was still determined to go straight to full-time university because I knew if I stopped, I might stop for good. I couldn't lose my momentum. Together, my parents and I came up with a plan that I'd go to the local university, and it would be all hands on deck to help me.

After I graduated from high school in May, I had another revision knee surgery in July and then started college at Arizona State University in August. On crutches. Breastfeeding a newborn. I was quite a sight.

A dear friend I'd known from church and still kept in touch with, Deanne, offered to take Nicholas during the day while I went to school. It was an amazing gift, and I am forever indebted to her. I'd drive to her house between classes to breastfeed, then go back to school. I was doing the best I could balancing school, a baby, and working thirty hours a week as a pharmacy technician. At first I was still living with my mom, but after saving some money and with the help of my dad, I was able to get an apartment for the two of us. My schedule was full, but I loved being a mother.

While studying for my degree in microbiology, genetics proved to be the most difficult course for me. During my third year of college, I had been studying for weeks while preparing for finals. I was exhausted, physically and mentally. Nick had just turned three. One day, he had a fever, which likely meant another ear infection, because he got them frequently. I came home from work at the pharmacy early to be with him. He was inconsolable. No matter what I tried, he kept crying. That went on for hours. When his fever spiked to 104 degrees and he wasn't responding to anything I was doing, I took him to the emergency room. It was scary to see him that sick, and I felt helpless because I couldn't make him better. We were there for several hours through the night, but after an IV and some stronger medications, Nick's fever finally started to come down and the staff sent us home around four in the morning. Thankfully, we both fell fast asleep in his red fire engine bed as soon as the sun started to come up.

A few hours later I woke up and was relieved to see my little guy still sleeping peacefully and no longer in pain. That was when my phone rang.

A friend asked, "How did it go?"

I started talking about Nick and what had happened at the emergency room, filling her in. There was a long pause at the other end. "I'm glad Nick is okay, but I meant, how did the genetics final go?"

I looked at the clock—the exam had taken place early that morning. The drama of the night had erased it from my mind, and I had slept through the whole thing.

I was in shock; I couldn't speak. My entire body started shaking with panic. I had worked so hard the entire year, struggling through the class to barely get a B. I knew the final would make up a significant portion of my grade, and without it, I would likely fail. I had blown it. I could barely breathe, and I started crying. I was so tired that my body felt numb, and I just sat there for an hour, staring into space. I didn't know what to do. Once I had calmed and accepted in my mind that I had failed the class and was trying to come to terms with it, I called my dad and told him what had happened. He said, "You need to go talk to the professor."

I told him that the professor was not the understanding type and wouldn't care. I was convinced that my fate was sealed, setting me back from my graduation date.

My dad asked, "At what point in your life have you been told that something was impossible and then you didn't try to make it happen anyway? Why would you just accept that there's no chance?" He also reminded me that my son needed me more than anything, especially the night before, and if being with him meant I didn't graduate on time, then that's okay. He said all the right things to help me reject defeat and reach out to my professor.

At midday, I went to his small, cluttered office. He was just as old and gruff as I had described to my dad, and after I asked if I could still take the exam, he refused. "You missed it," he said. "You can take it next semester."

I felt broken and without the energy to protest. As I slowly walked out the door, head hanging low, he stopped me. "Are you that girl who was standing in the back of the classroom in the beginning of the semester holding a kid while trying to take notes?"

The big lecture auditoriums usually hold at least two hundred students, so he didn't know us individually. However, one day when I had exhausted all my options and couldn't find a sitter for Nick, I had asked him before class if I stayed in the back and we were quiet, would he grant permission for Nick to be with me so I could attend his lecture. Surprisingly, he had allowed it.

I nodded. "Yes, that was me."

He peered at me for a beat and said, "Be back at two this afternoon, and you can take the final. You won't get full credit, but I won't fail you if you pass it, either." Someone I had thought was a horrible person actually wasn't when it really mattered. It was another significant moment that kept me moving forward.

I passed the class, and with a couple more years of really hard work, I graduated from college in four years. Once again, Nick was there when I received my diploma.

I was so proud of myself for graduating, but I didn't revel in the moment for very long. My focus immediately shifted to medical school. I had anything but the perfect premed application. I knew when compared to those of my peers, my application made me look subpar because it wasn't full of perfect grades and an abundance of volunteer work. Reminiscent of what had happened four years earlier, some people told me to forget medical school and start working. Others were saying to take the year off and do things to boost my medical school application. But they didn't understand how tired I was, and I knew that if I stopped, I might never start again.

I applied but was only wait-listed for MD programs. I had a good GPA, but when it came to the high bar for medical school, I fell short. I could have studied more and done more research activities, but then I wouldn't have been able to work and provide for my child. I would have spent even more time away from him during such precious years. Being wait-listed felt like a failure, but I knew I had made the right choice to prioritize my little boy. So if I couldn't get into an MD school, I decided to interview at osteopathic schools. After all, my primary care doctor was a DO, so I was familiar with the alternate route.

When I told my grandmother "Mommom" my plan, she was surprised and asked, "Is that still a real doctor?"

She didn't mean anything derogatory by the comment; she just didn't know. But it stuck with me, and I realized I needed the MD. My grandmother's approval meant the world to me, and I had always had in my mind that I would become an MD. Why stop now? I had no idea what to do, so I went to my immunology adviser to ask her advice, and I am so glad I did. She told me about an offshore medical school in the West Indies owned by a US company that accepted a large incoming class with less stringent entrance requirements. However, it was rigorous and there was a high attrition rate; up to 50 percent of students dropped out in the first few semesters.

It was a difficult decision to make. I had to decide if I was going to move to the West Indies and leave everything I knew behind, including my family and friends, to pursue getting the MD. Once again, instead of judging me or throwing water on my dream, my parents told me that only I could make the decision and they'd stand by me whatever I did.

So off we went.

The Rock

My parents flew to the island with me and Nick, who was now four years old. Ross University School of Medicine was located on the island of Dominica, and believe me, it wasn't like the Caribbean islands I had seen in television commercials; it was more like Jurassic Park. We referred to it as "the rock" because of its tall mountains and thick brush. I was terrified. Even though my parents helped me find an apartment and set it up, once that was done, they had to leave, taking Nick with them.

It was devastating. I had never been away from my son, and everything I had done up until that point was to be with him. I knew it was the only solution at the time, but still I cried for two days straight alone in my "new," run-down apartment. I would be attending four semesters without any breaks, essentially the first two years of medical school condensed into fifteen months. I couldn't keep Nick with me given the academic demands. Where would he go to school? Who would watch him while I was in class and studying? I didn't see how it could possibly work. In Arizona, I'd had my support group, family, and friends. Now I was in a foreign country, and I didn't know a soul.

It was tough. My parents and siblings and Nick's dad all stepped in to help take care of him that first semester. Banding together made it feel as though we were an unbreakable family unit, even if not in the traditional sense. My parents became close and functioned like teammates. Though they didn't rekindle a romance, they developed a deep friendship. Now they travel together and my dad hosts an annual Mother's Day brunch for my mom. Their commitment to our family in spite of their differences astonishes me.

Even with the comfort of knowing the family unit was intact in Arizona without me, I still didn't want to be away from Nick. So after I adjusted to the island a bit, I started formulating a plan. First, I managed to enroll him in the school that the professors' kids attended. Though he could be in school while I attended lectures, that still left the problem of what to do with him when I had to study in the evening. I went to my dean and asked if I could study in the library during the day instead of attending classes. That would leave the evenings free for some much needed mommy-son time.

At first he balked. But I pleaded. He realized that for me, it was not worth being in school if it meant continued separation from my son. He finally said, "If you can get straight A's the first semester and demonstrate you're a strong academic student, then we will consider it."

He gave me the biggest motivation of all: being with my son again. I told my parents the plan, and I'll never forget calling to tell them my final exam results. There were 130 questions, and I missed only one. My dad gave me a hard time asking me which question I had missed, but I knew he was proud. So was my mom. So was I. It was the first time I had gotten straight A's since becoming a mom.

I flew home after the first semester and took Nick back to the island with me for the next one. I had worked so hard to get good grades that I had barely seen the light of day. My parents thought I was too thin and looked sickly. I was just happy to see my little guy; it was as though a piece of me had been restored. Nick spent the next year living in the West Indies with me, and it was quite an adventure for us both. He played with kids in the local community and went to school on campus with me daily. I would love to say that it was easy, but it wasn't. I would tutor for extra money every chance I could get. Each time a storm hit—and they were frequent—we lost power and I studied in the humid heat by candlelight while Nick slept next to me. The storm would also leave us with brown water in our sinks and faucets for days, so we would have to carry water in jugs from the school water fountains up the long, steep dirt road that led to our apartment. But we were happy. I had also found a Catholic community on the island. It felt like a warm blanket wrapped around me every time I went in and heard the choir. I had always loved that feeling in my home church, and I was happy to have that familiar feeling again in such a foreign landscape.

Be Your Own Advocate

After completing the core medical curriculum, the next step of medical school is two years of rotating clinical specialties in hospitals and outpatient centers, taking the knowledge students have learned from books and applying it to real-world situations. There was one problem: the school's hospital relationships were in New York. Even though my plan had always been to eventually go east, there was no way I could be a single mom and a medical student—working long hours and not getting paid—in such an expensive city. It wasn't my time yet.

I would have to go back to my support system to continue the path from point A to point B, no matter how circuitous. Unfortunately, the school had no relationships with the hospitals in Arizona where my family and friends were. Instead of accepting the situation, I decided to lobby the local hospitals myself. Between the endless hours of studying for the medical boards, I acted like an insistent used-car salesman: I just kept at it, selling myself, writing letters, showing up, and begging whoever would listen to please let me do my rotations there. Every response was the same: "We don't usually accept foreign medical students, but after your boards, let us know your scores." Some were friendly, while others scoffed at me for being an offshore student.

I had gotten straight A's that entire year and a half on the island. When I took my boards upon returning to Arizona, I scored in the 99.7th percentile of all medical students taking the exam, US and foreign students. I wasn't inferior to the US students, and I had the scores to prove it. The other students weren't any smarter or better than me just because they had gone to an in-country medical school and I had been wait-listed; we had different circumstances and took different paths, but they ultimately led to the same destination.

After I submitted my scores, the local hospitals invited me to do most of my rotations there. I was elated. My first day at the hospital was also Nick's first day of first grade. We took a picture together to commemorate the special day that we were experiencing together.

I had late-night and early-morning shifts, so Nick and I lived with my dad for a while. Two years later, in 2008, I graduated from medical school with highest honors. Nick was once again by my side at the ceremony. The only person missing was Mommom, who had died the year before I graduated. She never got to see my name with MD after it, but it was her dying that led me to choose my specialty.

After graduating, it was time to select a specialty and apply for a residency where I would spend the next six years training for it. My grandmother had been diagnosed with late-stage breast cancer while I was in medical school, and after she died from the disease, I decided to spend my career advocating for early detection of cancer. Losing my grandmother was heartbreaking. I cried for weeks knowing that I would never be able to call her again to ask advice or get comfort. At the same time, I had a renewed sense of drive to do all I could to save people so they wouldn't succumb to the same fate she had. And this time, all of the big-name schools were coming to me because of my board scores and grades. I was offered residency interviews at all the top-tier programs.

Once again, my maternal instincts kicked in. Nick had just turned eight, and a medical resident works eighty to a hundred hours each week, with frequent thirty-hour shifts. Who was going to watch Nick overnight if I moved to New York City or Boston? Even though going east was still my plan after all those years, in my heart I knew it still wasn't time. I cried a bit as I canceled all the big-name interviews that I was so proud to have received. I'd thought if I landed a spot in one of those programs, I would finally be finished proving to others that I was worthy; that being a teen mom hadn't made me less. It was hard to let them go, but I did. Fortunately, I was able to secure a spot in the radiology program at our local hospital in Arizona. It was not as prestigious, but it was twenty minutes from my parents. The next five years of residency were going to be challenging, but I would still get to the same end goal as if I had gone to one of the other programs. I had my family and Nick, and that was really all that mattered.

It's Time

While doing research at Mayo Clinic in Scottsdale during my residency, I met my future husband, Paul, while he was in town for a medical conference. He was a brain surgeon doing his endovascular fellowship training at UCLA. Paul finished all of his training soon after we met and moved to New York City, where he was from. Even from three thousand miles away, he was trying to get me to go out on a date with him. His persistence paid off, and a year later I flew to New York so he could take me on our first date. We've been together ever since.

Despite our being in a long-distance relationship, after a couple of years of dating, he whisked me away to Saint Lucia, where he dropped to one knee and asked me to marry him. I didn't know at the time, but before our trip he had met with my dad and Nick to ask both for permission to marry me. We married in 2012 in an intimate outdoor ceremony surrounded by our closest family and friends. After we said our vows, we started planning our future while I was in the last years of my residency. I was a bit unsure how Paul would fit into the tight family unit we had developed over the twelve years since Nick had been born, but I longed for a partner. I had been busy for so long; I hadn't realized how much I was desiring another kind of love—until I met Paul. His ability to make me laugh and get me out of my apartment for some fun brought a lightheartedness to my soul that I don't think I had felt since before I became a mom. And his love for me was palpable.

Paul decided to leave his medical practice temporarily and move to Arizona so I could finish my residency—and during the last year of it, in 2013, Hudson was born. He brought such joy into our home, and it was wonderful to see Nick become a big brother. He loved it.

He would come home from school and hold Hudson while doing his homework. Soon after, I finished residency, passed my radiology and radiation physics boards, and started my Women's Imaging fellowship at Mayo Clinic.

As my fellowship came to an end, it was time to complete my lifelong goal and head east, finally making it to the point B I had envisioned as a teen. Paul's practice was there, and I had a job waiting as well. My friend Michael was right: I might not have taken the straightest path, but I still made it.

Upon graduating, when I was eight months pregnant with Harrison, we packed everything up and moved Nick, an infant Hudson, and a ninety-pound chocolate lab named Murray across the country—all cohabiting for two months in an extended-stay hotel because our house in New Jersey wasn't ready for us to move into.

Once Harrison was born, we settled into our home and figured out our new routines. In a matter of a few years, my household went from Nick and me in our small apartment to a family of five across the country from the family unit we had relied on so heavily before.

I would be lying if I said it was a smooth transition. Nick was not happy to leave Arizona and not thrilled about gaining a stepfather. It was a tough transition for all of us. In addition to normal adolescent hormones and emotions, my young teen was faced with moving away from his friends and extended family, starting at a new high school without knowing anyone, and having two young brothers at home taking up my time. It had been just the two of us for so long. Now my attention was divided among three children and a husband.

The cold, dark months of that first winter were difficult. It was good to see Nick working on new friendships at school, but I hadn't started my job yet and didn't have many local friends. I was also beginning to experience strange new symptoms affecting my eyes and various joints. Later, I would be diagnosed with an autoimmune disease, but at the time, I attributed it to having a third child and moving to a new climate, so I ignored the symptoms for years. My days were filled with caring for a colicky newborn, a vivacious toddler, and a moody teenager. The last fourteen years had consisted not only of caring for a child but also working on my professional career, so I always had a piece of me that was separate from motherhood. My new job wasn't scheduled to start for seven months after Harrison was born. I started to feel as though I were losing a bit of myself. I slipped into what now I believe was a mild postpartum depression.

Michelle recognized it, and so did my mom. Once again, Michelle came to be by my side and flew out to stay with me for a few days. Both younger kids were sick at the time, and she helped me clean up vomit, held my hand, and reminded me that it's okay not to feel on top of the world at all moments. She really is the best. Both of my parents also came for frequent visits, and Paul flew my entire family out to surprise me for my birthday.

In early spring, as the days started to become longer and the tree buds started to turn a reddish hue, I made the conscious decision to come out of my own winter hibernation along with the rest of nature. I started the new job and involved myself in the local community by joining various organizations, trying to make human connections and meet people. That was what pulled me out of the darkness that was beginning to envelop me. Being active, meeting people, getting outside your comfort zone can all feel impossible when you have hit a fragile low, but often, putting yourself out there is better than any medicine that can be prescribed. Doing so is ultimately what got me to my current job and how I made my way to FOX.

At work, I advocated on behalf of patients and partnered with state legislators in Arizona, New York, and New Jersey to ensure access to early breast cancer screening for women. It can mean the difference between life and death, and in the case of my Mommom, she had found her breast cancer too late. As I began to gain notoriety in the crusade, Memorial Sloan Kettering Cancer Center offered me a job—to help open its new site in New Jersey and assume the role of director of breast imaging there. Of course my answer was yes. I joined the world-renowned cancer center and have split my time between the main campus in New York City and the New Jersey site ever since. I still can't help but think of all the tears I shed because I feared I wouldn't make it east or be accepted by a prestigious academic center. Yet here I am.

Onward

At a social event a few months before the highly anticipated 2016 presidential election, I spoke candidly to a group of people about the Affordable Care Act, various health policy topics, and advocacy efforts. When there was a doctor in the crowd, people always asked what their opinion of "Obamacare" was. Well, my unfiltered opinion got the attention of someone who worked at FOX, and to my surprise, I was asked to go on *FOX & Friends* to discuss health care policy the following week.

My first interview was with morning anchor Ainsley Earhardt. I was so nervous I thought my heart was going to jump right out of my chest. But Ainsley is just as sweet in person as you'd imagine her to be from watching her on television. Her kindness immediately put me at ease. After that appearance, I was asked back regularly and soon after was offered a position as a medical contributor.

My role at FOX was amplified in 2020 during the covid pandemic. People were scared and confused, and I feel honored that I could contribute during such a terrible crisis. Nick came home from college when things shut down, and the five of us were back together again under one roof. All three boys would sit together doing their remote learning while Paul and I were still working full-time in the hospital. The boys were quite the threesome: Harrison in kindergarten, Hudson in second grade, and Nick a college sophomore. Although it was hard on the kids to miss their usual routines, the unexpected by-product of lockdowns and remote learning was wonderful family time together for us. When school and work were finished, we would play laser tag outside, hop into the pool, or simply watch a movie together. I hated the lockdowns, but I didn't mind the extra time with my boys.

In the last several years, countless strangers, patients, friends, and my own family have told me how much my words, either on television or in my books, impacted them and helped them through difficult times, Covid and beyond. Their comments fill me with a sense of joy that is indescribable and remind me that I can only see so many patients each day in the hospital, but I can reach millions more through my advocacy and media pursuits.

You're Perfect to Me

I am proud of my professional accomplishments. I don't need to prove anything to anyone anymore. I made it. Even though it didn't always feel like it, as Frank Sinatra sang, "I did it my way."

But my beautiful family is my real achievement. That is what makes me who I am.

Some days I feel as though I'm on top of the world, juggling a busy husband, three kids, two dogs, a full-time doctor job, and extracurricular activities. Other days, I feel as though the world is on top of me.

It's natural to try to do a million things at once, but I had to learn early on to be creative with my time to ensure that my firstborn always felt my love. I try to do the same today for all my boys. I have found a few ways to keep things organized in my mind and in my world. If you look at the calendar section in my phone, I have a dozen appointments each day for tasks I must get done, from signing school permission slips to doing academic research edits to scheduling a television interview. When those tasks are in my brain, they are jumbled and can be overwhelming. I will get to all of them. But instead of having them swirling inside my head continuously, I physically remove them by writing them down so I can be present in whatever I am doing at any given moment.

I try (not always successfully) to give my all and be as present as possible wherever I am. I certainly can't be in more than one place at a time, despite how much I want to or how hard I try to be. It has taken me a long time to realize that perfection is not attainable. If I try to be everywhere all of the time, I am not really excelling at anything I am doing. That's when things start to slip. My family, my patients, and I deserve more than my half attention. We deserve it all. When I'm in the hospital, I try not to think about my son's upcoming soccer game; that's not fair to my patients. When I'm at my son's instrumental concert, I try not to look at biopsy results on my phone, because that's also not fair. Everything has a time and a place. I will always get from point A to point B, but timing is everything.

It took a while, but the relationship between Paul and Nick has grown into something that I'm grateful for and means the world to me. Though the stepfather/stepson relationship started out a bit wobbly, both have become better versions of themselves and now seek each other's opinions and approval on many aspects of life. It just took a little time and growing up for both of them to find their way.

My two little boys, one in middle and the other in elementary school, are keeping me as busy as ever. At the same time, I am watching Nick start on his own path now that he has graduated from college. It's hard to believe he's all grown up, and I couldn't be more proud of him. Nick was by my side at all my graduation ceremonies—from high school through medical school and beyond—and we are all proud to watch him succeed as he pursues his dream of being an airplane pilot. Even though he's making his own way now, he still calls me nearly every day, and I hope that never changes. He has been a constant my entire adult life. I pray that I have given him—and both of my other children—the same unconditional love and support my mother gave me.

There have been times over the years when I questioned whether I had been a good mom and made the right choices for Nick. There were even a few years of Nick's life when it felt as though he hated me. When people say the teenage years are tough, they aren't kidding. It certainly was for us, but like everyone else, we got through it. Nick and I grew up together. He saw my strengths and my weaknesses, and he knows I'm not perfect.

So it means the world to me that in just about every Mother's Day card, he writes, "Mom, you're perfect to me."

CHAPTER 2

Janice Dean

Senior Meteorologist, FOX News

"To be honest, I never planned to be a mother."

Prior to joining FOX, Janice had already made her mark on her first love, radio. After graduating in radio and TV broadcasting from Algonquin College in Ottawa, Ontario, Canada, she became the morning show cohost, reporter, and even DJ at local radio stations in Ontario. Pursuing her American Dream, she left Canada and headed to the United States, spending time as a host and reporter on various radio programs until making her way into television and becoming one of the best-known faces of *FOX & Friends*.

When Janice was diagnosed with multiple sclerosis in 2005, despite facing a life-altering personal storm, she did not stop pursuing her professional dreams. In fact, her journey helped create the incredible person she is today. Since her diagnosis, Janice has become one of the biggest advocates for people suffering from multiple sclerosis, a mother of two boys, a *New York Times* bestselling author, and the creator of the successful children's book series Freddy the Frogcaster.

As a mother myself who also lives with an autoimmune disease, I have been in awe of Janice's openness about living with a chronic illness and have personally benefited from listening to her advice on how to share certain aspects of her health with not only the public but her family as well.

Radio Days

The trajectory of working in broadcasting was the organic path I was meant to follow. I am blessed to have this career in TV, but my roots are in radio. With radio, I can tell a story using my voice, and people can use the power of their imagination to visualize the pictures. There is something quite magical about using the imagination when hearing a story. I have enjoyed this since I was a young child. Before I could even read, I spent hours in the basement pretending to be on the radio. My mom would tell you that as a young girl I was always with a wooden spoon, interviewing anyone I could find. My dad even hooked up an old-fashioned tape recorder that had headphones and a huge microphone attached to it. Since my parents read to me a lot, I would memorize some of my favorite stories and then recite them into the tape recorder to listen to it, with *Alice's Adventures in Wonderland* being my favorite. I just loved the sound of my voice telling a story.

Because of this love, I studied radio and TV broadcasting in college and, when I graduated, started working in radio in Canada. It was a dream come true. Then one day I was approached by a news director at a local TV station in Ottawa, my hometown. He said, "Would you like to fill in for our meteorologist when he goes on vacation?" And I remember thinking, "That's a little out of the box." But I'm also the kind of person who loves to try new things, so I jumped at the chance. Back then, you weren't required to have the meteorology background that you do now, so I would fill in doing the weather occasionally. I did that for a few years. That was my first step into weather broadcasting.

When I came to FOX twenty years ago, I was looking for a reporter position. The boss at the time said, "I already have an entertainment person, and I don't really see you as a hard news anchor. Have you ever done weather before?"

I was excited to say, "As a matter of fact, I have."

Growing up in Canada, we had epic snowstorms, and I was always wondering how the forecasters knew how much snow we were going to get. Devastating ice storms ripped through the neighborhood and impacted my life; power outages lasted for weeks. There was one time the National Guard had to come in. Not only did the weather fascinate me, I saw firsthand how important it is for people to be alerted by meteorologists when there is bad weather coming. In that moment, it seemed, the person to do it was me.

That was a pivotal moment in my life. Though I had filled in doing the weather on occasion, it wasn't something I'd thought to pursue actively or that would be my eventual profession. Yet there I was being offered an opportunity, and I decided to take it. But I didn't just want to fill in anymore; I wanted to be better. I decided to go back to school in my mid-thirties to study meteorology while also working at FOX in New York City.

My future, literally, was in the stars.

American Dream

Also written in the stars was my husband, Sean, and the life we would eventually build together. To be honest, I never planned to be a mother. I was so focused on achieving my professional goals that family life wasn't at the front of my mind. I am sure a lot of people say that, but really, I didn't think about building a family during that time. I was busy chasing other dreams.

Shortly after I moved to New York in 2002, my friend Lianne was in Hawaii on her honeymoon. As fate would have it, while on a hike, she and her new husband met a nice guy named Sean who also happened to live in New York City. A fireman, Sean had lost many of his colleagues in 9/11. That had made him realize how short life could be, so he had set out to do things he had only dreamed of doing; surfing in Hawaii was one of them. The day he met Lianne, he was unable to surf because of the weather. The surf was too high to go into the water, so rather than wasting the day, he made his way over to Kauai to go for a hike. Talk about serendipity. As they all hiked together, Lianne told him about her friend—me—who had moved to New York and didn't know anyone. He gave Lianne his number and told her I could contact him.

Meanwhile, she worked on me as well to call him. The last thing I wanted at the time was a boyfriend. I was so focused on my career and learning to navigate the new city that I didn't really have the time, but she insisted, saying, "You don't have a lot of friends there. Sean can be your friend." And she finally convinced me to call him.

Sean and I met for breakfast in December 2002, and we both tell people it wasn't love at first sight. That's not a bad thing. Sean was someone I really liked talking to, and I had been in the city only three months. He became my first real friend in New York.

He said, "I can't imagine moving to a brand-new city and not knowing anyone." Born and raised in Brooklyn, he started showing me the best places around to hang out. As we spent more time together, a friendship began and grew strong. The difference between Sean and other men I had spent time with was that with Sean, it was just easy. We had no expectations other than being friends; love was the last thing I was anticipating. I think that served both of us well, because he wasn't ready for love yet, either.

About a year into our friendship, I realized that something had changed. We had gone out to dinner at a Belgian café and were drinking beers, eating French fries, and just laughing. I remember going to the restroom and it hit me, and I said to myself, "Wow, I *really* like this guy." After that night, I knew my feelings had changed. And it seemed that so had his. Hanging out slowly turned into dating in the most natural way. I like to say that the weather brought us together because it did; had the surf not been high on that day in Hawaii, our paths might never have crossed.

The Next Chapter

In 2005, my health took a turn for the worse. I could tell that something didn't feel quite right, and after some time and many tests, my doctors gave me a diagnosis that I had never expected: multiple sclerosis (MS). Multiple sclerosis is an autoimmune disease that affects the central nervous system, causing various symptoms such as vision problems, muscle weakness, numbness, fatigue, and even cognitive difficulties. Though there is still no cure for MS, there are treatments that help with the symptoms and can prevent new attacks. So I began taking daily injections to treat the disease.

Life went on.

It took a few years, but Sean finally proposed. Soon after we were married, my MS doctor asked if we were planning on having kids. I was already thirty-seven at the time. We looked at each other and said, "*Are* we planning on having kids?" We hadn't spoken much about it before then, so the question caught us off guard.

In a way, the doctor asking about whether we wanted to have kids was one of the best things that ever happened to me, because I'm not sure we would ever have talked about it. I would hope that we would have, but that moment pushed us forward.

We tried to get pregnant right away because I wasn't getting any younger. And just like that, I got pregnant at thirty-seven and had my first son, Matthew, in January 2009. I had a lot of morning sickness, but it didn't matter to me because it was a really beautiful time. I couldn't believe I had someone growing inside me. I was going to take care of that new life. It was a brand-new mindset.

After I stopped breastfeeding Matthew, we tried for another one. We were thrilled when I got pregnant again quickly. We saw the heartbeat on ultrasound and started wondering if we were going to have a boy or girl.

After a few weeks I knew that something was wrong because I started spotting. When the doctor did the ultrasound this time, the heartbeat was gone. It was devastating. I remember calling Sean and bursting into tears. My heart was broken. It was really tough, but my ob-gyn said to try again, so I decided to keep moving forward. Sean and I talked about it, and even though it was hard to grieve the child we had just lost, the possibility of having another one got us through, and we decided to try again.

We soon got pregnant and held our breath. We were so thrilled that my second son, Theodore, was born without complications in February 2011, two years after Matthew. I was almost forty-one, but we were hoping for a third child. Unfortunately, it wasn't in the cards, and again, I had a miscarriage.

Our wonderful ob-gyn said we could try again through other avenues such as in vitro fertilization. Sean and I talked about it, but the second loss had been even harder on us emotionally and it was just too difficult going through the grieving process again. There's no way to describe the anguish and the loss that you feel when you miscarry a child. I am thankful to have had my husband. Sean, as always, was my rock.

Even though I was sad, I realized that I already had two miracles, my beautiful boys. I didn't want to be sad for my kids; my biggest priority was Matthew and Theodore, and I decided to hold my head high and focus my attention on them.

Write a Letter

After having Matthew, when I got pregnant with Theodore, I wondered how in the world I would have the same amount of love for this next baby. Because when you have the first one, you are filled with this incredible amount of love that you never knew existed. It seemed impossible that I would be able to have that same amazing love again. And how could I share my love with another child? I felt guilty that I wouldn't be giving all my attention to my firstborn and worried that my love for Theodore would take away from my love for Matthew—and vice versa. They were interesting and conflicting emotions, and I didn't know how to handle the way I felt.

I had a dear friend who suggested that I sit down and write a letter to Matthew to explain the incredible love I have for him because he introduced me to the amazing world of motherhood. Just because there would be a brother or sister in his life, the love I have for him would never change.

It was a cathartic exercise that helped me so much. I wrote a two-page letter while I was bawling my eyes out. I'm getting emotional thinking about it even now, explaining my overwhelming love for him and thanking him for the gift of making me a mother. I still have the letter I wrote to him and plan on giving it to him someday— I'm not quite sure when yet, but probably when he's a man or when he's about to experience fatherhood.

Someday I'm going to write a letter to Theodore, too. My boys are the two halves of my heart, and that will never change. Even though I didn't choose to walk away from a career and become a stay-at-home mom as my own mom did, I strive to be the kind of mother she has always been, making sure her children feel loved and prioritizing us over everything else. Now that I have my own children, I have a new appreciation for her and the sacrifices she made for her family.

Honesty Is the Best Policy

It took a while for me to talk with my children about my MS because I wanted them to be old enough to understand. I believe that

God took care of that, opening the perfect path and creating the perfect timing to bring it into their world.

In third grade, Matthew's favorite teacher was Mrs. Kline. One day, Matthew came home from school and said, "Mom, there's something I want to tell you. Mrs. Kline is in a wheelchair." He told me about something she had said in class that day: "I may be in a wheelchair, but it doesn't mean I can't do the things I love to do. Teaching is what I always wanted to do. It's my favorite thing. MS is not going to stop me from that."

As he told me the story I had tears in my eyes, and I said, "Buddy, there's something I have to tell you. I have the same thing as Mrs. Kline."

He wasn't afraid or upset, he just asked, "Mom, are you going to be in a wheelchair, too?"

I answered honestly, "Maybe someday, would that matter to you?"

Without missing a beat, he said, "No, because look at Mrs. Kline, she's doing everything she ever wanted to do, and so will you."

I get emotional thinking about it; her wonderful impact and courage as a role model helped him have no fear so I could talk with him about having the same illness without scaring him. I was amazed and inspired by his teacher's positive outlook and my son's gentle heart accepting her.

When Theodore got to third grade, he also had Mrs. Kline, and we had the same conversation. He was just as kind and loving as Matthew. I am lucky and grateful to have these boys in my life. Now I believe that the reason I'm on the planet is for my family and to be a mom.

So in my house my kids know Mom has an illness, and they know the triggers; for instance, I can't be out in the heat for a long period of time. So that means that in the summer I can't do a lot of outdoor activities. I couldn't go to the Memorial Day parade recently because it was ferociously hot outside. So Sean went. We make a good team.

Even though I know it's best to be open and honest with my boys, there are moments when I'm not completely truthful because my instinct to protect them takes over. I don't want to look weak or have the boys worry about me, so I don't always tell them when I am not feeling well. But I should. I recently had a flare-up, and I kept it from them. I didn't tell them I was going through it. As a result of the flare-up, I was very short in attention and conversation with Matthew. He got upset and asked, "Mom, what's going on, what's happening?" I realized that he thought I was mad at him because I wasn't acting like myself, when really I was trying to protect him from seeing me in my condition. I felt bad that he felt he had done something wrong when he hadn't.

So I said, "Buddy, I need to be honest with you. I'm not feeling well, I'm going through an MS flare-up, which happens sometimes." That made me realize that I don't want to hide it from them. Honesty is the best policy.

There are things I'm going to miss because of the illness, but they know I'm going to make it up to them in different ways.

As Mrs. Kline said, she's doing everything she wanted to do. So will I. My advice is, don't be afraid to be married or have kids or chase your dreams or do that fun thing you always wanted to do. And try to be honest with your kids about what's going on with you. Let them love you as much as you love them.

It's worth it.

CHAPTER 3

Allison Deanda

Speech Therapist

"It's okay to fall apart sometimes because you're not going to fall apart every day."

When gathering stories for this book, I knew I wanted to talk to Allison; her unwavering determination and strength as a mother in the face of overwhelming challenges continue to inspire me every day.

I met Allison in November 2019, when she came in for a routine mammogram. She had had a benign lesion removed from her breast the year prior, which had brought her to Memorial Sloan Kettering, where she continued coming for her breast cancer screenings.

While she was waiting for her mammogram, we struck up a conversation as I was washing out my salad bowl. Neither of us knowing what the future held, we spoke about the ages of our kids and their activities as two moms, not as doctor and patient. We had no idea that the day would hold a moment that would change her life forever.

After her images were taken, I looked at them and noticed an abnormality. I promptly arranged for an ultrasound to further evaluate her breasts, given her dense breast tissue. After reviewing all her images, I decided to go into the room and scan the area myself. We had a full schedule, but at that point, I was convinced that something was wrong. Allison was only forty and had three little kids at home. The last thing I wanted to do was send her home to wait for a biopsy appointment.

I told her I thought that a biopsy was necessary. She got up to get dressed, but I said I wanted to do it that day. She was surprised but agreed.

The next day, I received the biopsy results, and my suspicion was confirmed. I called Allison to share the news. She wasn't surprised; she told me I needed to work on my poker face, that she could tell by my eyes that day it was cancer.

The day I told her of her cancer diagnosis was horrible for her, and the next three years would continue to challenge her. I admire how this mother has continued despite all the obstacles that continue to be thrown her way.

Just Remember, to Them, You're Mommy

For as long as I can remember, I knew I wanted to be a mother. I met the man I would marry when I was thirty. Before even getting engaged, we both said we wanted to start a family right away. We married in 2012, and two years later, I gave birth to twin daughters. I was excited to be having twins because I also am a twin and know how special that bond is.

Before the pregnancy, I was working full-time as a speech therapist for the New York City Department of Education schools. I finished the school year while pregnant, but because of a complicated pregnancy and frequent hospital stays, I was told to start my leave earlier than expected.

It wasn't an easy pregnancy. I had a lot of bleeding, and one of the twins' amnions was missing an important vessel that is essential to supplying nutrients. Because of this, she had intrauterine growth restriction. The doctors explained to me that my body had to work harder to get her everything she needed. As a result, I developed preeclampsia. I cried all day every day. I was a basket case. I didn't feel well, and I was terrified for my babies. Thankfully, my parents and husband were there to reassure me.

The twins, Bryn and Alex, were born in September 2014 and had to stay in the neonatal intensive care unit for ten weeks while they continued to develop. It's really hard to leave your newborns at the hospital after giving birth, but I knew that was where they needed to be. I was thrilled when we could finally bring them home.

When they turned one, I went back to work with mixed feelings about leaving them. It was hard leaving every morning, but honestly, some days it can feel like a minivacation to go to work when you're at your wits' end with kids and housework. I was fortunate because my parents watched them for me every day, and I imagine it's easier leaving your babies with their grandparents than with a stranger. It's a relief to know that they're in a good place—and a huge help financially, because child care costs are so exorbitant.

Two years after my girls were born, I had my son, Timmy. Life was good.

Then Memorial Sloan Kettering Cancer Center came into my life. In January 2018, I had a scare when a lesion was removed from my right breast. Thankfully it was benign, but because of my family history, I became vigilant with my annual cancer screenings.

In 2019, I was on my way to Sloan Kettering for my routine mammogram. I had left work early, and when I crossed over Red Hill Road into the parking lot, for whatever reason—I can't explain why—I had a weird, foreshadowing, terrible feeling. I shook it off and went inside for my mammogram. When we went on to do a sonogram, it seemed normal to me because of my dense breast tissue.

I started to get concerned, however, when the ultrasound technologist stayed in one spot for a very, very long time. In the past, it had been common for the radiologist to come in to talk, so I wasn't surprised when Dr. Saphier came in the room. But then she told me there was a spot on my breast that she wanted to biopsy that day. That was when my concern morphed into real fear; typically, I just made an appointment and came back if I needed more images or a biopsy done. Clearly, this was more urgent, and Dr. Saphier was emphatic: she wanted to do it that day. As a speech therapist, I do a lot of work with children on social skills, so I'm hyperaware of body language. When I saw the look Dr. Saphier gave the tech, I could tell that something was really wrong. After the biopsy, Dr. Saphier promised she would call as soon as she had the results, and I left.

I held myself together until I got to my car and then started crying hysterically. I said to myself, "She's going to call and tell me it's cancer."

The next day, the phone rang during my break at work, and I answered. Even though I had told myself I knew what was coming, when I finally heard Dr. Saphier say the words "It's cancer," I wasn't mentally prepared at all. It felt as though my whole world came crashing down at once. How could this be happening? I was only forty; I had little kids.

I immediately thought of them, not what type of cancer or what the treatment plan entailed. It was all my kids, my kids, my kids. Nothing else was running through my head. The twins were only six, and Timmy was just four. I didn't want to leave my kids motherless as my grandmother had when she died young. They were so small, the thought of leaving them consumed me.

The moment we hung up the phone I called my mom. As always, she was comforting, rational, and calm. She said, "We'll talk when you get home. We're going to have a plan." All I knew was that she would be there with me through it all.

When my husband got home, he was in shock, I think. I was more worried about the kids, trying to figure out how to tell them.

I had no idea how to tell my kids or how they would handle it. It's frightening to be ill, but on top of that, you're scared how your illness will affect your kids. I had a conversation with Dr. Kirstein, the surgeon Dr. Saphier sent me to, about how to go about it. Something she said really stuck with me. She said, "It's your decision if you want to tell your kids or not. I have patients who do both. Just remember, to them, you're Mommy. You're their safe space. And if you talk to them and give them the facts of what they need to know on their level, they might be less scared, because if we tell them nothing and you're sick or you keep saying 'I have to go to the doctor' or your hair falls out, they're going to be scared and create their own story in their imagination."

So I worked with a social worker at school. I wrote out a script, and I practiced it for a week because I wanted to get through it without crying. I also went to Barnes & Noble and got the books *Cancer Party!* and *The Nowhere Hair.*

A month after my diagnosis and a few days before starting chemotherapy, I told the kids. I read the books with the kids, and afterward we talked. Someone had said not to use the word "medicine" because if the kids saw me get sick when I took the medicine, they wouldn't want to take medicine ever again. So I used only the word "treatment."

I said, "Mommy has something called cancer. It's in my breast. The treatment might make Mommy not feel well some days." Then I told them that my hair was going to fall out, and that seemed to upset them the most. I understood how they felt; when the doctors had explained what would happen to me during chemo, all I'd heard was the Charlie Brown teacher in my head. They had said a lot of important things, but the only thing I had heard clearly was "You're going to lose all your hair." I imagine my kids felt the same way as I did.

My son said, "I don't want a bald mommy."

Ultimately, my daughter Bryn loved my bald head and rubbed it. Being autistic, she was determined to focus on the facts, because she does better when she is given information in black and white. So the *Cancer Party!* book was great for her; it explains how one cell decides to have a party and grows into cancer. It also discusses how the hair grows back and even how you can wear fun wigs. Bryn would also tell a bunch of jokes to make me laugh. That was her way of coping. I started a Facebook page and posted all her jokes on it to commemorate them all.

Alex, my other twin, had a very hard time with it all. I put her into therapy a month after my diagnosis so she would have an outlet other than me to help process everything that was going on. I think that was helpful.

The night before starting chemo, I was so nervous. Despite people trying to tell me about it, I didn't know what to expect or how I was going to feel. The next day, my husband took me to the first chemo infusion.

Other than during covid, when visitors weren't allowed, my mom, dad, sister, brother, or friends were with me. I always had someone.

After chemo I'd feel okay for the first few days, and then nausea and all the rest would set in. On those days, I was lying on the floor, sick, in the bathroom. Several months later, after I finished chemo, I was ready for surgery and had my mastectomy.

Cancer Party!

The back of the *Cancer Party!* book had ideas for how to help your children during cancer treatment. So I made a big magnetic chart for them. Every day I would post how I felt.

Today is a good day, Mommy feels okay. On days like that, the kids had magnets with activities written on them to choose from and we could go do something outside or get ice cream.

Mommy doesn't feel good today. On days like that, they could choose from other magnets with activities, such as snuggle, watch a movie, read a book. It was a lifesaver, because it gave them the feeling that in that scary circumstance, they had control over something. I have since given that board to others with small kids. Having kids is hard. Dealing with cancer while having kids is even harder.

Alex was sad and cried a lot throughout my treatments. I felt terrible for her, and my heart would shatter when I saw her tears. Sometimes I would cry with her.

She said, "I don't want to make you cry."

I told her, "Sometimes we feel sad, and crying is okay. Mommy is getting better and stronger every day."

I tried to reassure all of them the best I could.

Alex asked me a lot, "Are you going to die?"

I'd always say, "Not today." I didn't want to lie to them, because I didn't know if the treatment would work. Once you have cancer, there is always a chance it will return. Even though everything is moving in a positive direction, you still have that voice in your head saying, "It may come back."

During the workup for my breast cancer, I had a PET scan that revealed suspicious spots on my kidney and thyroid. The doctors didn't think they were related to the breast cancer and the breast cancer took priority, so I didn't have the other spots worked up for a few months. That was about the time the world was shutting down from covid-19. I just remember praying, "I don't want to have another surgery."

After my breast surgery, I met with the kidney doctor, Dr. Smith, and the first words out of his mouth were, "Your whole kidney has to come out. Even if it isn't cancer, it's overtaking everything."

I remember crying in his office; he was standing in the doorway at an awkward distance; it was March 2020, two days before everything shut down, and social distancing had started. My mom was there, thankfully, but that was the last appointment she would be able to come to for a while. After that I would be on my own.

After some more tests, I was diagnosed with kidney cancer and thyroid cancer, too. I asked my mom, "Why does this keep happening?"

And she said, "We are going to get through this."

Once again, my mom was my everything, taking charge. As she was asking questions and taking notes, all I heard was the Charlie Brown teacher in my head again. Thank goodness Mom was there.

During covid and the September 2020–2021 school year, I worked remotely and helped my kids with their remote learning.

Meanwhile, it was time to take care of the other cancers now that I had finished my breast cancer treatments. First, my kidney was removed. At the time, the hospital allowed only one visitor at a time, and you had to register that person before they could come in to limit the number of people in the hospital at one time. Having cancer is never easy, but having cancer during the covid-19 pandemic added another level of challenges.

Some days all I could do was cry.

Once I recovered from the kidney surgery, it was time to have my thyroid cancer removed. I made it through the thyroid surgery, too, and although I was tired of surgeries and recoveries that followed, I was grateful for my doctors. I was grateful to be cancer free.

However, although I survived cancer, my marriage did not. But after all I had been through, I wasn't scared to be alone. I thought to myself, "Look at all the things I did; I beat cancer three times and took care of myself and my kids through it all."

No Evidence of Disease

I went back in person to teach during the 2021–2022 school year. After everything I'd been through, it was good being back. It was also nice to be out of the house and see the kids I had been teaching remotely. Teaching speech therapy virtually had been awful. I finally felt a sense of normalcy again.

Eventually we learned more about why all that had happened to me. The geneticist called to tell me that a gene mutation I had had led to something called Lynch syndrome, which means I have a high risk of developing many different cancers. They presumed that my grandmother had probably had the genetic mutation as well, given that she had been so young when she died of cancer. My mom, brother, and sister were tested, too; we all have the mutation except my sister.

The hospital genetics department tests thankfully revealed that the kids' father doesn't have the gene, so the kids don't have to be tested unless they're having symptoms or until they're eighteen.

After my Lynch syndrome diagnosis, I chose to have a preventative hysterectomy to decrease my risk of developing uterine, ovarian, and cervical cancer. Right now, I am considered to be NED, short for "no evidence of disease," and I'm thankful. I still have another ten months of oral chemotherapy for my breast cancer to reduce the risk of it coming back. I also have follow-up appointments every three months for my various cancers and will for a very long time.

Some days the hardest thing for me is knowing that I can go only minute to minute rather than looking ahead to the future. I had always been a jumper, jumping months ahead in things. But I realized that I can't always do that now and need to take things a bit slower. I have no idea what the future holds. I also learned that it's okay to fall apart sometimes because you're not going to fall apart every day, so on the days you do, it's okay.

I don't feel the same as I used to. I am more tired while doing everyday things now. Some days I look at myself in the mirror and ask, "Is this real? Did all of this actually happen?" Other days I look at myself and say, "I can't believe how strong I am."

I want my kids to know that I am still me and will continue to be strong for them; after a treatment I can throw up, brush my teeth, wash my face, and say, "Come on, let's go outside and play." Some days you may not have the strength to do it, but other days you just have to pick yourself up and go because that's what you want them to see. You don't know if there will ever be a day when you won't be with them, so you need to be there as much as you can while you can.

That is my plan. I will be here for them as much and as long as I can.

PART II

Faith

God has a plan for everyone. Sometimes His plan for us takes time and patience to manifest itself, but it always does. Often, unexpected events will make us question if we are making the right decisions in life. But Faith is trusting the unseen.

CHAPTER 4

Ainsley Earhardt

Cohost, *FOX & Friends*

"God kept telling me, 'I have my hand on your life.'"

To most people, Ainsley Earhardt is the *New York Times* best-selling author and enchanting, familiar face on the number one morning show on cable news. To me, Ainsley is a dear friend. It's not that I don't admire her many career achievements, but it's her maternal instincts and light within that I hold in highest regard.

I never cease to be amazed and inspired by Ainsley's strong faith and steadfast ability to take a situation and find the silver lining in it, no matter how hard it may be to see it at the time. It was her hope and warmth that helped get me through my own darkness recently as my family was challenged emotionally and physically when one of my children was given an unexpected medical diagnosis. Ainsley was one of the few people I confided in regarding what my family was going through. As she tends to do, she leapt into action, sending warm food our way and reminding me that hope is never lost when those around you are praying for you. Her words and prayers brought such comfort during a very difficult time. I'm grateful not only for her friendship but for the ways she's helped me gain perspective, particularly as a mom, many times.

Let Ainsley Be Ainsley

Psalm 103 says, "The life of mortals is like grass, they flourish like a flower of the field; the wind blows over it and it is gone, and its place remembers it no more."

I love that scripture. To many it might sound depressing, but this life is not about us, it is about building the Kingdom of Christ for eternity. We're just here to serve Him and make a difference in the lives of others. My life story has ups and downs, but God has been good to me, so I want to share the hard times as well as the good times to help other people who may be struggling to understand why God is allowing them to be in certain situations.

My mom loved raising me in South Carolina; South Carolina was just who she was. She didn't have it easy, that's for sure. She was diagnosed with type 1 diabetes at age thirty-nine and suffered all kinds of medical complications because of it. But she never complained. She always kept her head up and continued doing everything for our family. I see that now, but I didn't appreciate it when I was younger.

We didn't grow up with a lot, but we had everything we needed. Mom taught preschool classes all day, and when she got home, she prepared a home-cooked meal for when Dad pulled up to the house. Sometimes he was stressed because he didn't enjoy his job, but come dinnertime, my family gathered around the table to say the blessing, and then we talked about our day.

Until I was a mom, I didn't realize how hard we were on her. She labored over a meal, and I'd say, "Mom, I don't want chicken Divan tonight because of all the mayonnaise. Just grill me a plain piece of chicken, and I'm going upstairs to study in my bedroom."

Instead of arguing with me about such a small thing, my mom would just do it. She didn't get angry, and she didn't make me feel bad; she prepared what I wanted. She was such a selfless caretaker in our family; she was special, and I was a typical teenager.

My mom was quiet and never wanted to be the center of attention. She loved working with children, but whenever she was nominated for teacher of the year, she did not want the award. She didn't want to have to give a speech because she was terrified of public speaking. She also tried to avoid joining a Bible study because she was afraid that they'd ask her to pray aloud. She eventually faced her fears.

Because we didn't grow up with wealth, traveling overseas was unheard of. So when my mom's cousin invited her to go to Scotland and learn about her heritage, it was a big deal. My mother saw *Cats* when she was in London and came home with a vinyl LP of the cast musical recording. One of my earliest, fondest memories is playing that record in the living room over and over, dancing and singing along with them.

I was very different from my quiet mother, and she always gave me room to, in her words, "Let Ainsley be Ainsley." I think in no small part because of my mother, I ended up in New York City and subsequently on TV because of it. And thankfully, my mom was able to see my success.

From early on, New York was where I wanted to live and TV was what I wanted to do. When I was little, I enjoyed going to the theater and taking part in all types of performance arts. I loved being onstage and knew I wanted to be on camera and entertaining in some capacity. I don't want to sound as though I only wanted to be famous—I just loved entertaining people. It came from a good place because, I think, it's just who God created me to be.

Mom had her moral boundaries and expected me to have the same. She kept me grounded and helped me make decisions. Obviously, the Lord led me, but my dad and mom were always the voices in my head directing me. I knew I didn't ever want them to see me in a situation where they would have been disappointed.

I'm just grateful for my parents' dedication and all the time they poured into our lives. Because when we're young, we think they don't do enough. "Oh, they're not at my recital" or "Why can't they be at my game?" We're hard on our parents growing up, and then later, we realize how fortunate we were.

Mom said the most important gift you can give a child is autonomy, and I'm very grateful she gave me that gift, so I could grow into my own person. But when I did need the important advice, she was always there.

No Looking Back

Growing up, I was taught that God gives you the desires of your heart. When you're young, you are convinced you know what you want for your life.

I was going to marry a wonderful Christian man and have a wonderful marriage. We were going to have children; we were going to pursue life together, love each other, and that would be enough.

But things didn't work out that way.

It was extremely difficult for me to admit and accept it. It was embarrassing that I couldn't make my marriage work the way I grew up believing you were supposed to. At the same time, God kept telling me, "I have my hand on your life, and I'm going to get you through this. It's not the way you imagined your life was going to be, but I promise you I'm going to make it better than anything you ever imagined."

And He has!

Yes, I wish I'd married the one man I met in college and he could have been the love of my life forever and we could have built a family together and been extremely happy, but that wasn't God's plan. It was *my* plan.

When I was going through my divorce, a friend of mine was also going through something unanticipated in her own life, and she said to me, "I never expected this, I never planned for this, but God showed me so many blessings with this and still has given me a wonderful life."

What she said really stuck with me. Sometimes it's hard to see parallels between certain situations, but they are there. I've learned the value of adopting that perspective through my own journey.

Rather than pushing hard for *my* plan, I needed to see that that relationship wasn't God's plan for my life. I can't spend my life looking back on it with regrets. I did love my husband, and we had many wonderful times together; we just went different ways. We are blessed with a beautiful daughter, and we are coparenting on the same page. Our only goal is to raise our sweet Hayden in a wonderful way and provide happy homes for her.

Let Hayden Be Hayden

My life may not be exactly the way I pictured it when I was younger, but I am blessed. I love my job and live in New York City. Dreams do come true. Mom would have loved it.

And I *love* being a mom.

Every night, Hayden and I read three books together. It's one of my favorite times of the day. I always include a book about the Bible, because Hayden loves learning about the characters and stories of the Bible. One day, Hayden went to her little Christian school and announced to the class, "We're all God's children." We had read about that the night before.

The teacher corrected her, saying, "No, only Jesus is God's child."

Hayden is a lot like me. She has a mind of her own and is eager to share her opinion. So she said, "I disagree. We are all God's children, and He created us in His image."

Around the same time, in the news, a little boy had a tragic accident with a whale. At night, Hayden and I talked about the news story, and it reminded us both of the Bible story of Jonah and the whale. The next day in school, the same story came up, and the teacher said Jonah hadn't really been swallowed by a whale.

"We are all God's children, and by the way, Jonah *was* swallowed by the whale," Hayden said.

What can I say? As my mom told me to be, I was proud of her autonomy and standing her ground.

Seasons Change

When Hayden was born, we lived in Manhattan, uptown on 72nd Street.

One day, a lady in my building told me, "I'm so happy for you having a baby! Let me tell you, as a mother, there are going to be so many seasons. Just know, some of the seasons are good, and some of them you will prefer to be out of, but they're all seasons. So when you're in a hard place with your child, just remember the next season is going to be great and you're not in that season for very long."

That was the best advice.

Right now, my favorite time of day is 3:15 in the afternoon. That's when I pick up Hayden from school. I never know what I'm going to get when I arrive; either she runs into my arms elated or she's crying because she's had a tough day.

Some afternoons, the season feels hard, but at the same time, I love that I get to embrace her at the end of hard days.

There's a verse I love, Jeremiah 29:11, that says, "'For I know the plans I have for you,' declares the Lord. 'Plans to prosper you and not to harm you. Plans to give you hope and a future.'"

That promise means a lot to me and helps me as I navigate life with Hayden. Hayden's seasons aren't always the ones I'd prefer to be in, but a new season is always around the bend.

I think about the scripture a lot, because I know that when I get a call from school saying that Hayden refused to participate in gym or she didn't do what the teacher told her to, they represent growing pains. Through the tears and hard times, I think she'll look back, as I did, and eventually realize that everything I did was because I love her.

In this season, it's true that I don't have a husband, and I would have liked to have more children. But I don't dwell on that. I focus on what I do have, my *many blessings*. Jesus Christ is my greatest blessing, and He gave me Hayden. I'm borrowing her from Him. My gosh, it makes me emotional just to say it because I'm so grateful.

I love being a mother. I love Hayden so much, no matter what the season. And I can't wait to see what the next one brings.

Always Watching over Us

I wish I had given my mom more praise growing up. I wish I had appreciated then what I appreciate now, that she did everything for us, and always with a smile.

In later years, my mom's diabetes caused kidney failure and she ultimately had to go on dialysis. When she suffered a stroke, it rendered her unable to communicate well for the last five years of her life. She tried to speak, but you could barely make out the words.

Both my parents had a strong faith, but Mom became an even stronger Christian later in life. And when she was sick, my dad was right there with her. I'm so glad they stayed together, and I saw how much they loved each other in the end.

During those last years, even though she was facing physical difficulties, Mom was always in a good mood and happy. She was almost happier than she had been in previous years. She was so close to Christ; thankful and always grateful.

I was in awe of her.

Now that I'm a mom, I think about all she did for us—with so much love and grace. And I understand it on a new level, because I have a little girl and I have a busy schedule and Hayden needs me regardless of that schedule. I appreciate my mom in the moments when I'm trying to get it all done.

I was there when she passed away on Saturday, October 22, 2022. I said to Mom through tears when she was at the end of her life, "I never told you this, but now that I'm a mom, I know how hard it is. I don't know how you did everything you did for me. I don't know how you worked and had three children. Being a mom is hard."

The Monday after she passed, I went in to work. It was something I needed to do. The viewers had been praying for her and sending letters with Bible verses of hope and comfort for years. Their prayers had kept her alive at times when the doctors had said she wouldn't make it.

Mom's friends watched, my family tuned in, and it was a tribute from us all thanking the country for their love and support.

The morning of the funeral, I did a *FOX & Friends* diner segment in my hometown dedicated to my mom; I knew that would have made her proud. The funeral was also a beautiful tribute to my mother and the life she led.

My mom wanted me to work no matter what; Mom and Dad never took time off and were always concerned if I did. At the time, there was a lot of news breaking, and I knew Mom would have wanted me to do my job.

But it's still sad to lose a parent. Sometimes the grief is excruciating, and I struggle with her not being here physically to hold on to. Even today, when I watch her funeral service again, I cry. It's okay to feel sad. I know it will take time for this fresh grief to heal, and I believe that day will come when all the wonderful memories will outweigh what I feel sometimes, even now.

At the same time, I know where Mom is: she's with her Savior,

Jesus Christ, and she's without pain, needles, dialysis, or surgeries. She is free and happy with so many people she loved who went before her, including her own parents. That gives me comfort.

My mother allowed us to shine, and she never received the credit. I told her so many times at the end of her life, "Thank you for letting Ainsley be Ainsley."

CHAPTER 5

Rachel Campos-Duffy

Cohost, *FOX & Friends Weekend*; Cohost, *From the Kitchen Table*
Podcast with Sean Duffy

"You would think that after nine kids,
being pregnant would seem more
routine to me. But honestly every baby
feels even more like a miracle."

The Bible tells us to "Love your neighbor as yourself." Following that scripture is easy when you are blessed with neighbors like Rachel and her entire Duffy clan.

I met Rachel years ago, when her husband, Sean, was still in Congress, well before she was the famed weekend cohost of *FOX & Friends* and she was flying into and out of New York City from their Wisconsin home. As luck would have it, when Rachel, Sean, and their nine children relocated east to be close to the FOX News studios, I was thrilled to welcome her to the small community in northern New Jersey that I had called home for the preceding ten years. Because of our close proximity, our friendship has grown, and I am fortunate to see her more in her natural, maternal role, outside our professional lives.

First, I'm amazed at how effortless Rachel makes being a mother of nine look. She and Sean are a cohesive team, and I admire their devotion to their family.

I also have great respect for Rachel's deep faith and her commitment to showing the world that people with special needs are an integral part of our society and not to be dismissed or forgotten. I remember sitting with Rachel in a FOX greenroom years ago when she was pregnant with her youngest. She confided in me that the doctors had told her the baby had heart defects and a high likelihood of Down syndrome. Even knowing that the future would be filled with many unknowns and at least a heart surgery for her newborn, Rachel exuded a sense of serenity as we discussed it. The future challenges were no match for the unbridled love she had for the child growing inside her.

Rachel has taken her experiences of raising nine children, including one with Down syndrome, and used her expansive platform to educate people about an often-misunderstood condition. There's so much I admire about her as a mom, but it's her passion for her children's well-being and her advocacy for other children's happiness that inspires me the most.

Faith and Order

My parents met when my dad, a Mexican-American airman stationed at a military base in Spain, fell for a local native girl, my mother.

My mom's parents were Catholic writers and intellectuals who took their faith very seriously. Her family had been deeply affected by the Spanish Civil War in the 1930s. Catholicism was very much under attack during that time, but their pro-Catholic stance never faltered.

My mom is very grateful for her faith and for her ability to practice it freely in the United States. She's also adamant about protecting that right because she has seen firsthand that the ability to practice your faith can come under attack.

She passed her faith and conviction down to her children, and I'm thankful for the way her influence has guided me throughout my life. The teachings and traditions of Catholicism, along with the personal experiences my mom has shared with me, have been my beacon and provided a road map for my marriage to Sean and raising our kids.

My mom is a "tough love" kind of mom. I think I'm a little softer, but I still have a bit of that in me. I run a tight ship. I have to!

I still remember how my mom made my siblings and me clean the house and always keep it tidy. We got in trouble if we didn't pick up after ourselves. And if our friends made a mess, we had to clean up after them as well.

I think that sense of order is another gem handed down to me because I'm like that in my own home. With nine kids, I need that order to manage everyone; I can't think if the whole place is a disaster area. It slows us down. If you can't find socks or shoes for the kids when you're trying to get out the door, that's a problem.

My kids know that their doing chores and helping to keep our space neat is necessary because our home is our sanctuary. If we don't have peace at home, we won't have it anywhere.

Don't Be Afraid

I know how blessed I have been with all my pregnancies because I never had to battle with fertility issues that so many women go through. All nine were unplanned but happy surprises for us. Valentina, number nine, was the biggest surprise of all. I was forty-eight, but after my other pregnancies, we were used to taking it in stride.

About five months into my pregnancy my doctor called me. "Hey, can we talk a minute?" she asked.

I said, "Yes."

She went on. "Are you sitting down?"

Again I said, "Yes." It was a strange request, since I thought she had called about an appointment.

She continued, "I need to let you know that the chances your baby is going to have Down syndrome is about ninety-nine percent."

The tests had also revealed several holes in the baby's heart.

I was taken aback at first. It was a lot of information at once. "Oh. Okay, thank you," I answered.

I wasn't upset about Down; I was more concerned about the heart condition. Our bandwidth as parents was already stretched thin. At that time, Sean was representing the 7th Congressional District of Wisconsin as a US congressman. I don't think people realize how intense or demanding it is to serve in Congress, especially with eight young kids. We had already moved to Wausau, Wisconsin, just to be close to the airport since he had to commute back and forth to DC three or four days each week. At that point, he'd been on that travel schedule for nine years, since he had first been elected in 2010.

I called Sean to share the diagnosis, and he could sense that I was a little discombobulated.

His response didn't surprise me—he has always been so great, open to life and kids and whatever happens. He immediately said, "Oh, that's no big deal; everyone we know who has a child with Down said it's the best thing that happened to their family."

And it's true. Sean's colleague representing the state of Washington, Cathy McMorris Rodgers, was one of those people. Her son, Cole, has Down. At the time, Cole was twelve and we had gotten to know him.

Instantly, our concerns lessened, and from there it was off to the races.

Of course, Cathy was one of the first people Sean told about our baby Valentina's diagnosis. She immediately sent us all kinds of books and resources. She even sent DVDs of *Life Goes On*, a great TV show from the 1990s portraying a family with a Down child named Corky. The actor who portrayed Corky, Chris Burke, also has Down syndrome.

Sean and I spent the summer months talking about what we needed to do to make sure this little girl would have everything she needed. We didn't know how much more she might require, but we knew we had to make sure we could provide it for her.

Sean thought it was a sign from God to let us know it was time for him to get out of Congress and focus more on our family. I was probably more against change at that point. We had always adjusted to the demands in front of us. I thought we would be fine if Sean continued in Congress. But Sean insisted, "No, we need to do this."

It was a massive decision—and it's the best decision we ever made for our family.

Sean has continued to make those decisions. A year after he stepped away from politics, there was a huge groundswell of people trying to get Sean to run for governor. But Sean was adamant. He kept saying, "My first job is dad. My first job is family. And I would regret missing this time. I won't regret whether I was governor or a congressman or not."

He's a wonderful guy.

I think one of the great blessings about Valentina coming along was that it made us really face our circumstances and how they affected our family. We had been feeling the strains of Sean's job for years. Her entrance forced our hand to make some changes.

It's good that we already had the nursery ready by the end of the summer, because we were in for another surprise. We were expecting Valentina at the end of October, but my doctor told me I needed an emergency C-section, and Valentina came into this world on September 30. She had already been tiny in the womb because of her heart condition, and now she was a month premature. Consequently, she was born even smaller than most premature babies are. After she was born, when I looked down at that beautiful little soul, her humanity was already so expansive, so obvious, it filled the whole room.

Just as Sean predicted, Valentina is the best thing that has happened to our family. She's so special and truly the light in the house. She is everyone's favorite family member—and usually the only thing we all agree on.

So if someone out there finds out during pregnancy that her child has a cardiac or other issue, or if anyone is feeling fear not knowing if you can handle it or what to do, I want you to remember one thing: Don't be afraid. Help is all around you.

Nine Is the Perfect Number

I do my best to educate people about Down syndrome and take the fear out of the diagnosis. But sadly, some of the fear comes from medical people, who should know better. I know firsthand that those with Down thrive—and instead of doctors and the medical community pushing doubt, there should be more discussion about the services and resources available to make it possible.

In 2022, the World Health Organization put out a tweet about Down, describing it as a "defect." I don't even know what that word means. I look at Valentina, and to me, she's perfect. I see a child, a human being. She's definitely not a defect. The more we talk about Down in a negative way, the more people are prejudiced against people who aren't "perfect."

Many young women have told me stories about being pressured to have an abortion instead of having a Down baby. We know it's true because it is estimated that 80 percent or more of Down pregnancies are terminated. In countries such as Iceland, the statistic approaches 100 percent. Iceland claims to have eradicated it, but Down is not an illness, it's a chromosomal variation. They haven't cured anything; they have simply exterminated those who have it.

Everyone has a different story, but for me, it never entered my mind to end my pregnancy. I'm pro-life and an opponent of abortion. You would think that after nine kids, being pregnant would seem more routine to me. But honestly, every baby feels even more like a miracle, and I am blessed with the ability to grow a child inside my body and give it life.

A year after Sean stepped down from Congress and Valentina was born, I was offered a job at FOX News, which turned out to be another blessing. When we packed up our family and moved to New Jersey to be closer to the New York studio, little did we know that the services for children with special needs in New Jersey would be spectacular. Thanks to the support of these resources, Valentina is flourishing.

I purposefully try to do stories about Down on *FOX & Friends* to dispel myths. I've met so many amazing people with Down, and each and every one is incredible because they have no malice. They just have *love*.

I see that every day with Valentina, too. When I take her to the FOX studios, she goes through the hallways—it doesn't matter who she meets or what they look like, she just hugs them. It could be Nicole, whom she knows and who has that mom vibe about her, or if she sees a stranger, such as the comedian Jimmy Failla, with his wild jackets and shoes, she gives him a hug, too.

Valentina does not discriminate against or judge people. She approaches everyone with openness, love, and curiosity. As the verse in Isaiah says, "A little child shall lead them." And she certainly does. If only more people would follow her lead.

We all have a purpose, and I see Valentina's every day. She makes us all better. My kids have learned to be more patient and help more, and that has built their character. They have become more aware of others with special needs. When we're out, they always notice who needs help and want to interact with them. My teenager Paloma volunteers for an after-school program for kids with special needs.

I think that's awesome and I'm proud of them.

God Knows What We Are Going Through

One year when we had six kids and my daughter Paloma was two years old, we went on a family vacation to Disney World. We intentionally split up for a ride; Sean took some of the kids with him, and I took the others with me. It wasn't until we reunited after the ride that we realized Paloma wasn't with either of us. It was one of the worst moments of my life. Even telling the story now, I can't explain the depth of the trauma.

She was probably gone for thirty minutes, but it felt more like thirty days. I was convinced that something terrible had happened to her. We had all our kids in a huddle to pray with Evita, who was twelve at the time, staying to watch her younger siblings while Sean and I looked for our lost little girl.

Disney World is big, but when you don't know where your child is, it seems infinite. Everyone suddenly looked suspicious to me, and I was convinced that somebody had taken Paloma. There were so many strollers; I just thought about how easy it would be to put a two-year-old into one of them, walk out of the park, and disappear. It was terrifying. In those moments, I made so many deals with God, praying for my little girl to return.

The Disney staff tried to calm me down, which only made me more upset. They kept saying, "Don't worry." They must deal with a lot of parents who lose sight of their children every day. But that didn't make me feel any better.

Eventually they located Paloma, and I was relieved when the staff told me she was waiting for us at the City Hall in Disney World. She had wandered away and walked up to a woman, who had stayed with her, trying to figure out whom she belonged to. I was grateful for that woman's kindness in helping her find us. When I finally had Paloma back in my arms, I didn't want to let her go.

Even though we had park passes, the next day we didn't go there. We stayed together at the hotel as a family. We needed a day to recover emotionally; the experience had been traumatic.

For a long time after that, I felt guilty. Really guilty. I had recurring dreams that Paloma was lost and it was my fault. I felt horrible and couldn't let go of thinking that I had been to blame, and all of a sudden I was questioning my ability as a mother.

One day I was praying the rosary. In the Joyful Mysteries of the Rosary, one of the last is the story of Joseph and Mary losing Jesus in the temple for three days. After all the dreams and worry and guilt, it was so reassuring to know that the Holy Family had gone through the same terror I had felt when Paloma went missing. Imagine that you've been entrusted with Jesus, the Son of God, and you lose Him! Reflecting on this story was a clarifying moment that resonated with me as a mom. Jesus' mom lost the Son of God for three days, so maybe I shouldn't feel guilty anymore. After that, I decided not to allow myself to be consumed with guilt, and the nightmares stopped.

Since then, I've thought about that concept a lot and applied it to my life on a much broader scale. It's comforting to know that Jesus went through everything we've ever experienced and will experience, whether it's shame, betrayal, death, grief, or other circumstances. As mothers, we go through every emotion from the peak of happiness to low valleys of doubt. It is easy to praise God during and for the wonderful times. And anything else I face has already been experienced by the Holy Family and can be addressed and healed through my faith in Jesus Christ.

CHAPTER 6

Emily Barron Smith

FOX Viewer; Prayer Shawl Creator
From her daughter, Juliet Hardesty

The Lord is my shepherd; I shall not want.
—Psalm 23

When I spoke to Juliet Hardesty, it was clear what an impact her mom, Emily Barron Smith, has had on her life—and so many others'.

When Juliet was diagnosed with breast cancer, her mother, Emily, knit her a special shawl, made with love and blessed by clergy, to provide warmth and comfort during her treatments. Emily took the act of comforting her daughter during a difficult time and turned it into a lifetime ministry, providing prayer shawls for those in her church community going through times of transition. We always say "It takes a village" to push through hard situations, and often we feel alone when we are struggling. Through prayer and dedication, Emily has proved that all you need is to perform an act of kindness to provide comfort during difficult times.

Family Is Important

The Silent Generation, those born in the years before the baby boomers, were most known for their traditional values, resilience, and self-sacrifice. It's as though the description of that generation was created solely based on my mom, who was born in Lexington, Kentucky, on August 18, 1931. Her generation is an amazing one that has a much stronger sense of community than what we are living in now.

Mom was raised a socialite; manners and etiquette were modeled and expected whether she was on a playground or attending a luncheon. Following in the family females' footsteps, she displayed dignity, for example wearing starched white gloves while shopping downtown.

Mom and her older sister attended the University of Kentucky, pledging Chi Omega, and their social calendars were full. Mom met Dad in a class upon his return to college at the close of World War II while he was serving in the Navy. She became his Sigma Chi sweetheart, and they were married following her second year of college. As avid Kentucky Wildcats basketball fans, they started a tradition that continues, with their season tickets enjoyed by all members of the family.

Dad's job at the Kentucky Utilities Company provided well financially for my parents. Together, they had many couples as friends, enjoying frequent parties and dancing at cotillion events. During the daytime, Mom found pleasure in community service, the women's club, bridge, family obligations, and social gatherings.

I was raised in a traditional southern 1960s family in which Dad was the head of the household. He arrived home Monday through Friday promptly at five-thirty, and the six o'clock news was ready on one of the three available channels. While being entertained along with Dad by *The Lawrence Welk Show* or other TV variety shows, Mom would keep her hands busy with crochet, knitting, or needlepoint projects. She delighted in the scripture-based illustrations and verses she needlepointed, and they were crafted into kneelers in our church.

At home, my brother, Pressley, and I were instructed on our place in the nuclear family and our roles; expectations were clearly defined, and respect and manners were essential. We ate as a family for every meal, and Dad would begin meals with "God is great, God is good, let us thank Him for our food."

For us to leave the table, we all had to finish before permission was granted. We had house and yard chores assigned without allowances given and were grounded if they were not completed. Those parental expectations taught us that with all involved and sharing responsibility, no one carries a heavier burden than another.

The importance of helping and enjoying family was instilled into us at a very young age. We could be seen digging up dandelion weeds in my grandparents' yard or hosting ladies' lunch at bridge parties. As a family, we worked *and* played together; family camping trips were a joyous adventure.

We also worshipped together. Christ Church Cathedral, an elegant historical Episcopal church, was our multigenerational home church. We all had special family pews used on Sundays, and Mom's needlepoint kneelers always graced them. We were Episcopalians from the cradle, and the church was our spiritual and social hub. Pressley sang in the choir, I taught Sunday school, Dad served several years on the vestry, Mom volunteered in Women of the Church, and my aunt was in the Altar Guild. The whole family was involved.

The whole family would also routinely gather at my grandparents' house for Sunday dinner. On Easter Sunday, regardless of age, children had to participate in the annual Easter egg hunt; all those from infant to twenty-one would fill a basket. We weren't a family that memorized scriptures or prayed much together, but we felt like we *lived* our faith; we showed it through how we embrace community and care for other people.

The Original Prayer Shawl

Sadly, my father died unexpectedly in 2011 from a brain bleed following a traumatic fall. The next year, when I was fifty-seven, I received more unexpected news. While teaching a small first-grade reading group in my neighborhood school, Glendover, my doctor rang my cell phone and I listened to her brief informational call.

A recent mammogram showed a cell mass that needed biopsy and now removal. After a deep breath and swallow, I finished the reading instruction with the class, followed by the principal excusing me for the remainder of the day.

Once I was in my car, my first call was to my husband, Mark. Then, with calendar in hand, I called the doctor, who provided me with information about the necessary tests and their dates. I was pleased that in the upcoming week we could still make our annual spring vacation trip to Florida. I had been doing that since high school.

Mom wintered in Florida, so as soon as I got there and we could embrace, I shared the news that I indeed had breast cancer. Mom is such a strong person; she did not cry. I, however, soaked my shirt with my tears. Once my vacation ended, daily updates were communicated to Mom until she arrived back in Kentucky in late May.

Surgery was scheduled for early June, after the end of the school year.

I think my mom wasn't sure how to take the news of my cancer, and she couldn't cure it, so she did what she always did: she kept busy using her hands. She prays when she is knitting, and therefore, her prayers are lifted in the little loops. Mom must have prayed especially hard, because the shawl she knitted for me is a long shawl. And just for me, she used various shades of pink with a breast cancer symbol and a Christian cross knitted into the stitches.

I turned to a friend at the Episcopal Church of the Resurrection outside Lexington for spiritual support for the upcoming journey. The rector, Reverend Jan Cottrell, had been a college mate, we were former vestry members, and she had presided over my wedding to Mark. One spring morning in the Bluegrass, four generations— Mom, myself, my daughter Katherine, and my grandson, Triston— met with Reverend Jan. After we chatted about my treatment, Mom shared the calling that she had felt to knit the shawl. We calmly followed Reverend Jan into the sanctuary. After draping the shawl over the altar, we gathered around to watch as she placed her hands on it and kneaded the fibers. As she prayed, the shawl seemed to swell, and my eyes teared. Reverend Jan charged each of us with an important role to care for me during this time. She talked to God about where we had been: how she had married me, how my journey had been transformed, and what there was ahead to face.

The long shawl engulfed my body as Reverend Jan placed it around my shoulders.

Holding Mom's hands, Reverend Jan prayed for all Mom does with her hands, saying, "Bless your hands and keep them safe as you continue this ministry."

June brought my surgery, with Mom and Mark ever present.

Before my postop surgery appointment, I was called back in to hear the news that additional surgery would be required; the doctor wanted to remove a greater margin, as I was HER2 positive.

I had no fear as I knew God was with me. I told myself, "It's going to be okay; you have to have faith and move forward." And that was exactly what we did. The next week, surgery was scheduled, followed by six rounds of chemotherapy and thirty-five radiation treatments.

Throughout chemo, Mom was with me for every appointment. So was her prayer shawl to cover me and keep me warm. I had a port catheter in my chest to deliver the medicine, and each treatment was an all-day event, so we needed to be clever with coming up with ways to stay entertained. My dear teacher friend Kathy, my mom, and I giggled and laughed, finding joy. My daughters, Beth and Katherine, would stop at the clinic during their available time. We cherished the bond of women being with one another. I got through the months of treatments with gratitude for the prayers and all the doctors' care.

Coincidentally, as I was finishing treatment, it was the same month as the Susan G. Komen Race for the Cure. Hairless and topped with a pink wig, I was escorted in a wheelchair through downtown Lexington among teacher friends, staff, friends, and family.

The shawl didn't promise healing or cure me of the cancer, but it was indeed a comfort throughout my journey. It lies beside my couch now, and I still snuggle with it often.

Ten years have passed since my breast cancer diagnosis, and I am grateful to be doing well.

Ministering Hands

After my cancer journey and the comfort Mom's shawl brought me, she said, "Juliet, I feel called to knit these for others going through a hard time." There were a few knitters at her Florida winter home church, and she joined in at St. Mark's Episcopal Church in Venice, Florida.

That began her lifelong ministry of being the leader of a group of women. In the weekly bulletin, individuals are invited to learn the art of knitting and/or enjoy the monthly fellowship. Some women are seasonal to Florida, while others arrive monthly, as Mom does.

Mom is selective of the yarn she uses; the colors used in each shawl must be complementary, and the softness of the shawl is of premier importance; therefore yarns are in-person purchases. Sale prices are always a bonus, enabling her to acquire a constant supply. Once the design is determined, with hands and needles ready . . . Mom begins a shawl.

Once a shawl is complete, Mom folds it neatly and tucks it securely within plastic, accompanied by a beautiful card. She feels that the Prayer of Comfort with its gorgeous artwork created for this ministry by a parishioner is as much a symbol of love as the shawl itself. Each shawl then awaits a blessing by the clergy. A large basket in the entry foyer is kept full of blessed shawls. There is always variety; some shawls are very feminine and some are masculine, and the colors range from vivid Florida tones to soft neutral hues. No two are alike. If you need one, you take it, or if you know of someone in need, you take one for them. Some shawls are even mailed out. Mom stops by during the week, making sure the basket is full so that the shawls are readily available.

Joy Shawls

After the success of her prayer shawl group, my mom wanted to do even more. She told me, "I'm doing these prayer shawls for an urgent or sad need, but what about shawls for joy and letting people know they're cared for when they're away? High school kids go off on their own and leave their family. They need to know they're still loved by their community and there's a church family here that loves them."

Now, every April, when kids are preparing to graduate from high school, Mom asks the members of her church who have kids graduating what their plans are. She then makes shawls in the colors of the various colleges they will be attending in the fall. She does not forget those taking the varied pathways of trade school and those going into the work force; she finds out what their favorite colors are and makes sure that they, too, have a shawl.

She didn't stop there. She expanded to wanting to provide shawls to newborn babies. That's her newest venture, and for the babies she is the pickiest about which yarn and colors to use. For accurate measurement, she used one of her great-granddaughter's baby dolls.

The Power of Prayer

It's amazing to me the way the power of prayer and how Reverend Jan's prayer years ago over my shawl and over my mother's hands has manifested in everything. At ninety-two years young now, Mom has no arthritis, her hands are still strong, and she continues to do her work. She drives herself to church, to the hairstylist, to the grocery store, and then to make prayer shawls. She even drives herself to the grief group she began years ago at the church after my dad died. She feels as though she needs to be there as a listening ear, even though she's not grieving anymore. The group members meet monthly, and if anyone is having difficulty, whether from losing a spouse or having financial problems, they all get together and share their stories and support one another. They listen, they pray, and sometimes they go out to lunch. She is always going somewhere.

The breadth and depth of the knitting she does can touch anybody. My mom is busy knitting at this very moment. She told me the lanai is warm but she has the fan on and is busy knitting. And praying. Always praying.

CHAPTER 7

Kayleigh McEnany

Cohost, *Outnumbered*

"Don't miss the moments."

Before Kayleigh came to FOX, I was familiar with her notable career in politics and her reputation as a media powerhouse. But it wasn't until the 2020 covid pandemic press briefings that I realized how impressive she truly is. During one of the most divisive and controversial times in our country's history, she stood tall on a national platform and handled disgruntled journalists as they desperately tried to rattle her. They couldn't.

Fast-forward to the day I interviewed Kayleigh by phone. She was juggling her infant son, whom I could hear babbling in the background, as she had just gotten home from hosting *Outnumbered* and was settling back into home life. She consistently demonstrates that amid chaos her ability to maintain a calm demeanor remains.

That isn't the only gift she has that makes her remarkable in my eyes. Kayleigh has accomplished so much. After graduating from Harvard Law School, she was eventually appointed press secretary in the Trump administration. She has also written three books, two while raising two kids with her husband, Sean. And that's only a partial list of her achievements.

Because of my career in breast cancer, I am proud of Kayleigh as she has become a strong public voice for women who are at high risk for the disease due to BRCA gene mutations. The way she has taken her personal experience of having the mutation and used her public platform to bring awareness to others reflects her strength as a woman and is a testament to her faith.

Wit, wisdom,
and prayers.

Love,
Mom

On Doubt

"Don't 'should'
all over yourself."
—Jennifer Hegseth's mom,
Linda Cunningham

"It's okay not to feel
on top of the world at all
moments."
—Nicole Saphier, MD

"There are so many
pressures on women, and
sometimes things just don't
work out. And that's okay."
—Carley Shimkus's mom,
Zulma Shimkus

The very hairs on your
head are all numbered.
Do not be afraid.
You are worth more
than many sparrows.
—Luke 12:7
(from Kayleigh McEnany)

"You have so much guilt....
I wish I had gotten rid
of all the mom guilt earlier."
—Amy Brandt

"We are all human, and stuff
happens; forgive yourself....
Don't worry if you
occasionally drop the ball."
—Martha MacCallum

On Feeling Overwhelmed

God is faithful, He will not
let you be tempted beyond
what you can bear.

—1 Corinthians 10:13
(from Nicole Saphier, MD)

"If I've learned anything in all
these years...it's this: Life gets
in the way of our plans."

—Jennifer Griffin

Come to me all you who are
weary and burdened,
and I will give you rest.

—Matthew 11:28–30
(from Nicole Saphier, MD)

"I learned the hard way that if we don't pay attention to our health and take the time to care for ourselves, we are not going to be there for the people who need us."
—Martha MacCallum

"Once you accept that the key to survival with dueling home and work duties is setting boundaries, your life gets a lot better."
—Jennifer Hegseth

Therefore do not worry about tomorrow, for tomorrow will worry about itself. Each day has enough trouble of its own.
—Matthew 6:34
(from Nicole Saphier, MD)

"Don't miss the moments."
—Kayleigh McEnany

On Believing in Yourself

"Don't wait for things to happen;
make them happen."
—Marion Champlain

"Don't be afraid to be married,
or have kids, or chase your dreams,
or do that fun thing you always
wanted to do."
—Janice Dean

"I decided I'd stop saying no to new
things out of fear. I made a pact with
myself: Just say yes."
—Annette Hill

"Go to the ends of the earth
for your dreams."
—Jennifer Griffin's mom,
Carolyn Griffin

Delight yourself in the Lord and He
will give you the desires of your heart.
Commit your way to the Lord;
trust in Him, and He will act.

—Psalm 37:4
(from Ainsley Earhardt)

"You can make anything happen,
and if you go for it, and fail,
so what? Just try something else."

—Marion Champlain

"As a mum, sometimes you just
know what's right for your child,
whether it makes sense to others or not.
There's no rationale; you just have
to listen to your instincts.
You get a bit of a sixth sense
with the people you love."

—Alicia Hall

"I made the decision that despite
the unknowns, I would have this
child—and there was no one who
could change my mind."

—Nicole Saphier, MD

On Building Character

Train up a child in the way he should
go and when they grow old,
they will not depart from it.
—Proverbs 22:6
(from Carley Shimkus)

"We all have a purpose.
Tell your kids that every day."
—Rachel Campos-Duffy

"The most important gift you give
your child is autonomy."
—Ainsley Earhardt's mom,
Dale Earhardt

"Try to be honest with your kids
about what's going on with you.
Let them love you as
much as you love them."
—Janice Dean

"Talk about everything.
Take too many pictures.
Keep all the letters.
Be grateful for every
single moment."
—Annette Hill

"My mom instilled in me early on
that family is everything. We should
be supporting one another."
—Sandra Smith

"My kids know doing their
chores and helping to keep our
space neat is necessary because
our house is our sanctuary.
If we don't have peace at home,
we won't have it anywhere."
—Rachel Campos-Duffy

On Allowing Others to Help

"It's okay—and very necessary—
to recognize that you need help
sometimes. So be sure to seek it
out when you do."

—Jennifer Hegseth

"It really does take a village,
whether you are in a crisis or not, to
raise children. And if you are faced
with one, you need all those people
around you. Strangers and friends."

—Alicia Hall

"We are all asking the same questions:
Can I have it all? Can I do it all?
The answer is no."

—Sandra Smith

"If I was facing something,
I knew I needed to tell my mom.
I had never been good at keeping
secrets from her anyway."

—Nicole Saphier, MD

"My family and few close friends who
were giving me a safe space, loving me
and believing in me, were my biggest
sources of strength."

—Nicole Saphier, MD

I am with you; do not be dismayed,
for I am your God. I will strengthen
you and help you; I will uphold you
with my righteous right hand.

—Isaiah 41:10
(from Nicole Saphier, MD)

"Good morning, this is God, I have it all
under control. I do not need your help."

—a quote taped on Jennifer Hegseth's cabinet
(from Dr. Wayne W. Dyer)

"I could not have processed my grief
had my mother not encouraged me
to reach for more, to try something
new, to push forward."

—Sandra Champlain,
Marion Champlain's daughter

On Faith

"It's amazing to me that the power of prayer has manifested in everything."

—Juliet Hardesty, Emily Barron Smith's daughter

For nothing will be impossible with God.

—Luke 1:37
(from Nicole Saphier, MD)

The Lord is my shepherd; I shall not want.

—Psalm 23
(from Emily Barron Smith)

"In the midst of pain, it's hard for us to see that all these little beautiful moments and signs in our lives are not just a coincidence. They are threaded together in a pattern, and when you look back on it, you realize God was always there."

—Annette Hill

For we walk by faith, not by sight.

—2 Corinthians 5:7
(from Nicole Saphier, MD)

"I knew God was with me.
I told myself,
'It's going to be okay;
you have to have faith and
move forward.'"

—Juliet Hardesty,
Emily Barron Smith's daughter

Bless the Lord, all His works,
in all places of His dominion.
Bless the Lord, O my soul.

—Psalm 103
(from Ainsley Earhardt)

"In an incredibly unlucky situation,
we can still find the light."

—Alicia Hall

On Inner Strength

"Some days you may not have the strength to do it, but other days you just have to pick yourself up and go because that's what you want your kids to see."

—Allison Deanda

God is our refuge and strength, an ever-present help in trouble.

—Psalm 46:1–3
(from Nicole Saphier, MD)

"I genuinely believe that people will be very surprised at how much they can deal with and survive. I was. It is within all of us to cope."

—Alicia Hall

"Getting outside of your comfort zone can feel impossible when you have hit a fragile low, but often, putting yourself out there is better than any medicine that can be prescribed."
—Nicole Saphier, MD

"Some days the hardest thing for me is knowing I can only go minute to minute rather than looking ahead to the future."
—Allison Deanda

"I needed to find a way to stop living in despair. So, I started a gratitude journal....If you're thinking only about awful things, they are all you're going to see."
—Annette Hill

Trust in God

My parents had an enormous impact on my life, not only because they are wonderful and kind but because of their strong faith. I grew up attending church on Sundays and youth group on Wednesdays. Faith was a constant part of our lives. Even in the car, I distinctly remember my mom playing Christian music and singing along to the words. I grew up watching my mother turn to God during trials and tribulations, and I admire her remarkable strength in doing so.

That was never more apparent to me than in 2009, during my senior year of college at Georgetown University, when my mom was tested for a mutation on the BRCA genes—a mutation that causes a higher risk of certain cancers, including breast cancer. Eight women in my family, aunts and cousins, had battled breast cancer, so we knew we had a strong family history. Mom tested positive for a mutation on the BRCA2 gene, which meant she had a nearly 84 percent chance of developing breast cancer in her life and a 27 percent chance of developing ovarian cancer.

She did not have cancer when the mutation was discovered, but the chance of developing it was so high that she wanted to know what she could do to lessen it. She decided to undergo a preventative bilateral mastectomy to bring down her chance of developing breast cancer to virtually zero. It was a brave decision.

I was only twenty-one when she did that, but her courage and determination were a guiding light, and I, too, got tested. I remember my doctor told me that I had tested positive for a mutation on the BRCA2 gene right near Christmastime.

My team of doctors recommended several ways forward, among them a preventative bilateral mastectomy. I knew that I wanted to follow in my mother's footsteps and undergo a preventative bilateral mastectomy, but I was too scared to go through with it right then. My risk of developing breast and ovarian cancer would rise precipitously after I turned thirty. My thought process was: "I'm not married yet. What will it be like to date after a double mastectomy?" So I delayed it for ten years. At the time, it made sense to me, but looking back, I realize those ten years were full of stress and apprehension as I wondered if my decision to wait was the right one.

Every six months I had a mammogram, an MRI, and oftentimes an ultrasound done as my breast tissue was so dense. Still, there were many false alarms, and I worried often.

I will never forget my mom calling me in May 2013 and telling me I had to go get a copy of the *New York Times*; Angelina Jolie had written an op-ed about her decision to have a preventative double mastectomy because she had a mutation similar to mine on BRCA1. I can't tell you what a relief it was to see someone so young and at the top of her profession writing about her thoughts and fears. I wasn't alone. It had a huge impact on me.

Soon after the op-ed, I met Sean, my future husband. After a while of dating, he proposed, and we married in 2017. He supported my decision to have a preventative double mastectomy and promised to be by my side throughout the journey.

So a year after being married, I mustered up the courage to have surgery. In the end, it was one of the best decisions I ever made. I'm blessed to have found such a wonderful man to share my life with and stand beside me during difficult periods.

Having kids was a desire that God put into both of our hearts. I wanted to be able to carry my own biological children if I possibly could. My doctors recommended that I wait to remove my ovaries until later in life, so I decided not to have my ovaries removed, even though I worried that by keeping them I would be at a higher risk of developing ovarian cancer.

Once again, I carried some worry with my choice, and there were occasional scares. Before both of my pregnancies, tests revealed what appeared to be a mass on one ovary. I went to my doctor and was petrified, but thankfully, both turned out to be false alarms.

Then came the blessings; both times, I conceived almost immediately after medical scares. That's where trust in God comes in. It's the idea that He knows me and has a plan for me. Blake and Nash, our two beautiful children, were part of His divine plan.

Trusting in God gets me through.

I'm so grateful to my mom and all the women who came before me who spoke publicly about testing for mutations on the BRCA genes. And even though I have chosen to keep my ovaries for now, I remain vigilant and trust that God will guide my path.

One in eight women will get breast cancer in her lifetime, so I want women of all ages out there to know that although it may seem overwhelming or you may be scared, get your mammograms and be proactive. If you have a family history of cancer, you may have a genetic mutation you could be tested for. Knowledge is power. And if you have any questions, you can always ask Dr. Saphier!

My Mom Is a Hero

In more ways than one, my mom has supported my career. She constantly encouraged me throughout college and graduate school and always believed, too, that God has a plan for me. I was able to achieve a lot not only because of the faith she instilled in me but because of her faith in me.

I was working on President Donald Trump's 2020 presidential campaign when I gave birth to my first baby. It was a crazy schedule, and I loved my job, but I was also overjoyed to be a mom. Of course I wanted to be with my little girl.

Campaigns are like a freight train gathering speed: they don't stop. You have a finite period of time to get the outcome you want; you're working toward a November deadline, and then that's it. You reach the goal or you don't, and it's over. Being a new mom on that kind of schedule was a challenge.

Right after Blake was born, I started traveling a lot for the campaign, and although I loved being on the campaign trail, I missed my baby.

My mom put in hero's work and made the decision to travel with me so I could take Blake along. I say "hero" because that was what she was to me. I remember boarding planes and my mom taking the wheels off the stroller while I was balancing diaper bags and carry-ons while trying to hold on to Blake. Once we'd get to the destination, I'd go to work and my mom would set up a makeshift crib in our hotel room and watch Blake for me. Though the job was exciting, my favorite time of day was at the end, when I would return to the hotel room and hold my baby.

During that time, the covid-19 pandemic hit, and the world started to shut down. So the travel portion of the campaign slowed. The silver lining was that I was able to be home in Florida and spend more time with my family.

In April 2020, I was asked to become part of President Trump's administration as White House press secretary. When I got the call, I was holding Blake. I remember thinking, "How can I do this and be a mom?"

I truly believe that God wanted me to do it. I knew that I needed to take the job, but it might mean not being with my baby every day. That was overwhelming. I started crying, and tears actually fell down onto Blake's little body as I held her. In that moment, she lit up with what I remember as her first smile. It was so sweet the way she looked at me, and I realized it was her way of saying, "Mommy, go do this." It was also God's way of saying, "I've got you. It will all work out."

Even so, I had a lot of fear. I left Florida in the middle of the pandemic to return to living and working in Washington, DC, and air travel was difficult at the time. I didn't know when or if I'd be able to go home and see my baby or if Blake would be able to travel to come see me.

Once again, my mom was a hero and snapped into action. She said, "You have to go do this. We will make sure you see Blake even if we have to drive up to bring her to you."

She kept her promise. A few weeks after I started the job, she was able to fly up with Blake. I'm so grateful to her and to my husband, who were both a huge help in making sure I could see my baby girl—and my baby girl could be with her mom.

He Knows You

As my children face the world, social media, and all the challenges we talk about on television daily, it is reassuring to know that God knows everything about them. He formed them in the womb and with a purpose. I'll share that with my children as they grow.

One of the big joys of being a mom is being able to watch how my daughter's mind works, the things she says. It's also amazing to guide her as she grows in her faith, just as my mom guided me. As I spent my childhood surrounded by the church community, Sean and I make sure we raise our family the same way. He's Catholic and I'm Southern Baptist, so we alternate between our churches, making sure the children are part of both communities.

Anyone who has gone to an evangelical church knows that

Evangelicals are a little more vocal during services, with many people praising Jesus' name all throughout worship. One Sunday, Blake was dancing around in the pew to the church music and a beautiful woman nearby kept saying "Jesus" over and over during praise and worship time. Suddenly Blake looked up, and had the most excited little face on. She asked, "Mommy, when is Jesus getting here?"

I thought it was hilarious but held my laughter and explained that Jesus was in her heart and everywhere around us at all times.

After that, when she would tell me that there was a monster in her bedroom or she was afraid of something, I'd say, "No need to be afraid. Remember where Jesus is?"

And she would point to her heart and say, "He's in my heart."

It makes my heart full every single time.

All Hands on Deck

Soon after my tenure in the Trump administration ended, I went to work at FOX. I'm able to work and be a mom because the support system I have surrounded myself with is phenomenal. Thanks to FOX's generous leave policy, we spent a lot of time with family in Florida after Nash was born. We were able to go to the beach and to the park and have a ton of family time without distractions.

We got to bond with our family and get to know our new son. My daughter is just like me as a child: talkative, vibrant, and always running around involved in something. My son is just like my husband: calm, sweet, and takes it all in. It's fun to watch my kids interact, and Nash just laughs at Blake's antics, mostly.

My main support system is my family—and it's a family effort all the way around to take care of the kids. It really is all hands on deck at all times with our career responsibilities while we are also parents. I watch the kids in the afternoon after cohosting *Outnumbered*, and Sean watches them in the morning. Both of our parents stay with us for weeks at a time to watch the kids and help when we need them. It's really wonderful that the kids get to spend time with Grandma and Grandpa because that is an important relationship. No one is going to love your baby as much as your family does.

Don't Miss the Moments

One recurring piece of advice I get from parents whose children have grown is "Don't miss the moments." That's a really powerful message. One day there's going to be a last diaper you change, a last onesie you put on, a last time you hold your baby before they walk. So I try to keep that in mind, and I now make my New Year's resolution the same each year: to always try to be present and not miss the moments. I want to take in all those special times because they won't last forever.

It's not easy, though. There are schedules and deadlines and so many things to juggle. Being a working mom presents many challenges. There are many times when you're doing a million tasks at once and you end up making comical mistakes. Sometimes there are moments when you just have to laugh at yourself.

During my second pregnancy, soon after starting my role cohosting *Outnumbered*, it was a busy news cycle and my mind was all over the place. I was taking care of a toddler while thinking about a new baby growing in my belly and going to work as well. I remember my husband calling me at work, sounding worried. "Kayleigh, are you okay?" he asked.

I said, "Yes, why wouldn't I be okay?"

He answered, "Because you left a pack of baby wipes in the refrigerator."

Somehow I had gotten distracted after I had opened the package and taken some out. Instead of putting the container back where it belonged, I had opened the refrigerator and put the baby wipes inside.

Those are the times to just laugh. I burst into laughter. So did my husband.

So when the day is packed or my mind is racing thinking, "I have to do X, Y, and Z," I have learned to say, "Put down your work and play dolls with Blake or cuddle with Nash."

There will always be another task, another impossible deadline. My children are my biggest blessing and gift, and time slips away too fast.

I don't want to miss a minute of it.

PART III

Purpose

The strength and drive women carry within them are expressed in many ways, whether in the pursuit of professional aspirations or the dream of creating a family. The road is rarely straight and smooth—rather, it is full of bumpy turns—but conviction deep within keeps us moving forward to reach our destination. But more important than the destination is the journey and finding the moments of bliss that are important—and more satisfying than we could ever imagine.

CHAPTER 8

Carley Shimkus

Cohost, FOX & Friends First

"I'm a brand-spanking-new mom.
I have less than a year under my belt,
yet it feels like an eternity because
my entire life is different
than it was just a few months ago."

Carley was at the tail end of her maternity leave with her newborn son when we spoke for this book. Naturally, she was experiencing all the emotions of a young mom anticipating leaving her child for the first time.

Anyone who watches Carley on the early-morning show knows she is an enthusiastic go-getter. This is absolutely true when it comes to her professional life. Years ago, when Carley started as a production assistant at FOX, she had a dream and went after it. With patience and hard work, she became the cohost of *FOX & Friends First* while also being the headlines reporter for *FOX & Friends*.

I met Carley well before her current host role. I remember having a soft spot for her because she and her husband were managing a long-distance relationship, a challenge I was familiar with. They kept up the long-distance relationship because of their jobs while dating, through engagement, and even during early marriage. When they decided to have a child, her husband made the decision to come to New York so Carley could continue to pursue her professional dreams and they could be a family unit. I couldn't be more proud of them for the way they handled their nontraditional, challenging situation. The selfless actions they both took in the name of love are inspirational. They are a special couple, and I know Carley will navigate the journey of balancing work and children with the same tenacity and spirit she brings to her career.

Love at First Sight

I met my husband, Peter, in 2009, right out of college in New York City. We hit it off instantly. He worked in finance, and with me being in the media world, we share a love of politics and current events, among other things. Meeting Peter was an interesting turn in my life because I had always been laser focused on my career and the dream of being a television host. I was constantly involved in student government throughout school and was so excited to be working at FOX.

But I also really liked the guy. I knew he was the one for me early on and I was going to marry him. Fortunately, he felt the same way. So we dated in New York for a few months—and then life threw us a curveball: he got a great job offer in Chicago that would require him to move there.

Neither of us wanted to end our relationship, so we decided to try long distance with the plan being for me eventually to go to Chicago. In theory that sounds as though it wouldn't be too hard to manage; love conquers all, right? But we found out quickly that it takes planning, commitment, and patience, not just passion, to build a life with someone even if you love them dearly. It's even harder if you are far away from each other and both focused on demanding careers.

But we were determined to try.

However, every time that I started to take a step to make that move to Chicago happen, I knew in my gut that it wasn't where I was supposed to be. I felt that there was something pulling me to stay in New York.

At the time, I was a production assistant at FOX, not making much money. And New York is an expensive place to live in. It would have been easier to leave and head to Chicago, but I knew that there would be more for me in New York. Peter was so good about it, too. He never got mad or pressured me; he knew how important that path was to me.

So after a few years, instead of walking away, Peter proposed to me, and we got married in 2015. I didn't think I could love him more than I already did, but his continued commitment to me despite the long-distance relationship made my love even deeper.

In 2021, I finally got my dream job. FOX named me cohost of *FOX & Friends First*. Just WOW! My career had always been the largest focus in my life, so when I reached my goal after all those years, I knew it was time to focus on my family life, because being a mom was another goal of mine. I was excited and a bit nervous when my husband initiated the conversation. He said, "Let's have a baby, let's start a family."

There was a lot going on, not to mention that I was now the anchor of a 4:00 to 6:00 a.m. show, which meant that I was working overnight.

But even though my career was pretty hectic, I wanted to be a mom and have a family with that wonderful man.

So since we were still living in different states, we came up with a plan. Trying to have a baby when you live far apart is a challenge; it takes a certain amount of planning and specific timing to get pregnant. We realistically knew that we could see each other only two days a week.

Once again, Peter was a rock star. If I was fertile on Wednesday, he'd fly in and fly back out on Thursday. Whatever day I was ovulating was our date night. It may not sound romantic, but it was wonderful. It made for some hilarious maneuvering sometimes, but to be honest, I was relaxed throughout the whole process because I believed it would happen when it was supposed to.

And it did. The next year, I was pregnant. Now we had some decisions to make. The long distance had worked when it was just the two of us, but soon there would be a little one in the picture, and that changed the equation. We decided to make another transition, and Peter moved back to New York.

The Next Phase

After I had my son, Brock, I went on maternity leave. The first month was a little harder than I'd thought it would be to fully recover physically. The second month was all about getting used to having a little baby and a schedule revolving around him. Around the third month, Brock started showing his personality—and smiling a lot. I have been overjoyed since.

Thank goodness for my own mom in those early months. She was—and continues to be—amazing. She stayed with us for the first three weeks after I came home from the hospital. We live in a New York City apartment—it's just two bedrooms. But that didn't stop my mom. She slept on an air mattress while helping me adjust to having a newborn son. It's definitely a memory I will never forget. Having Mom there was such a huge help for me and Peter, particularly for the middle-of-the-night feedings. The three of us took shifts feeding Brock. It was certainly a team effort.

I have always been grateful to be close with my mom, especially now that I'm a mom myself. Every conversation I have with her is filled with little bits of support and advice. She gives me advice on everything from how to change diapers correctly so they don't leak to little things that I will keep with me forever. Just recently she told me, "There is no such thing as holding your baby too much because they won't be this size forever. Hold them, love them as much as you can. It will never be too much."

Like many women, I had difficulty breastfeeding. I wanted to so badly, but it just didn't happen. My mom helped me let go of the disappointment and even the guilt by simply saying, "There are so many pressures on women, and sometimes things just don't work out. It's okay. That's why there is formula!" Sometimes a mom just knows how to make you feel better.

I also hit the jackpot with my wonderful mother-in-law. She is the most considerate woman I know, and her Memphis southern charm only makes her more endearing. As I transitioned back to work, she came to stay with us to help with the change. Though we offered for her to stay with us the entire time, she insisted that she stay elsewhere on the weekends to ensure that our little family had alone time, emphasizing the importance of those moments being reserved just for us.

I'm lucky to have two strong female figures in my life who are there for me and involved with Brock's childhood growth.

As Brock has gotten a bit older, my husband has gone back to work and fewer people are around, so I am enjoying the moments of it being just me and Brock. He is quickly becoming my favorite person to be around, always smiling at me and watching me whether we are in the gym together, running errands, or just sitting and looking at each other.

I'm a brand-spanking-new mom. I have less than a year under my belt, yet it feels like an eternity because my entire life is different than it was just a few months ago. Brock has already changed my life—and me—and the amount of love I have for him is indescribable. I know every parent thinks their child is the best, but I can't believe the magnitude of the love I feel. I am sure the hormones have something to do with it, but I could cry right now thinking about how much I love this precious little guy. I'm entranced with everything he does. The first time he moved his rattle from one hand to the other, I thought, "Can somebody please give this child an Oscar?" All the little joys of nurturing your child are gifts. You see this little innocent baby who needs you so much, and you think, "Oh, my gosh, I made that. I'm doing that, I'm cultivating that." It's magical. I now understand why my parents love me so much and do so much for me.

As my maternity leave came to an end, I began wondering what the next phase for our family would be. It is all uncharted territory. Because of our work schedules, we had to hire a full-time nanny to help care for Brock. That was scary. Dealing with the unknown and letting up on the reins a bit can be difficult, especially for new moms.

But as much as I love being home with Brock, I love being at my dream job, too.

I have so many different emotions about heading back to work: I'm excited, but I'm also sad and a little nervous, too. I'm afraid I'm not going to be able to sleep very much between my work schedule and a young child. When I return to work, I'll be heading into an election cycle, and my job will only get busier, so I will have to work hard to continue doing my best at work while making sure I am still the best mom to this little guy. I know I can do both. Thankfully I have a lot of love and support around me to make sure I do.

Richer than I You Will Never Be, I Had a Mother Who Read to Me

Looking ahead, it's exciting to think of all the things Peter and I can teach Brock and expose him to as he gets older. Peter played football at Princeton and is still very much into sports. I really hope he exposes Brock to all the sports he loves, so they will be something they can bond over and also enrich his world. And I certainly hope Brock gets his dad's athletic abilities because although I ran cross-country, I am certainly not what people would call athletic. Plainly put, I have a lack of coordination; it may be because of my height, or at least that's the excuse I give to myself. My husband believes that being part of a team community gets you away from the phone and gets you outside. In today's world, that is so important, so I will do what I can to encourage that.

I also want to pass along the joy of reading. Reading to Brock is one of my favorite activities. The book I love most right now is called *The Very Brave Lion*. I've read it to him countless times, and I get weepy every single time. I always think, "How can I still be crying over this story?"

The book is about a little lion whose father is the king of the lion pride. In the story, the dad tells his son that one day his son will take over as king. The little lion is nervous because he thinks he can't possibly do such an important job. But the father encourages him; he tells him he sees how his son plays with the other lions. He lets him know that he may be small right now, but he will grow up big and strong like his father. He lets his son know that it's okay to be frightened because sometimes he's frightened, too.

This message doesn't just apply to the father-son relationship; it applies to the mother-child relationship, too; that's why I love it. It reminds me of how I felt as a new mom and continue to feel every day. Everyone has insecurities; mothers worry if they're being good moms. And I love how the book illustrates a parent being there for the child and building them up. I know Brock will have moments of doubt in his life, and I will be by his side to help him overcome his worry and build him up when he needs it, just as my parents do for me.

A Good Foundation

As I grew up in Long Valley, New Jersey, my mom was a stay-at-home mom, totally hands on with me and my older sister. Though most people wouldn't associate New Jersey with being rural, with rolling hills and woodland, that was the serene environment I grew up in, and I hope to raise Brock somewhere similar—maybe just a little closer to New York City so my commute to work won't be terrible. Every night, our family ate my mom's home-cooked meals together. Being together around the table as a family is a strong memory of mine.

My family is very close, and a part of that is because of our faith. My parents are both very religious and instilled a strong faith in us girls as well. We went to church every Sunday and were an active part of our church community. The church youth group activities encompassed our entire social life, and we had a blast. I love looking back on all the fun activities we did as a community; it didn't seem like a big deal then, but it was such a positive experience that helped shape who I am today.

I think the religious foundation is missing for so many young people these days, and I really want Brock to grow up in a church community with a strong faith, as I did. I will do everything to be able to pass along the same values I learned and make sure he has that strong foundation of religion and faithfulness in his life.

In my bedroom when I was a child I hung a cross-stitch picture my mother made of Proverbs 22:6: "Train up a child in a way he should go and when he is old, he will not depart from it." At the time I thought that "train" referred to a choo-choo train. It wasn't until I was older and a mother that I realized the profound meaning of it. As moms, we are blessed with a human being whom we have the responsibility not only to care for but to make sure they become good people and continue spreading goodness in the world. This is a big job, and it will take family, faith, and love to get it all done. I am up for the challenge.

CHAPTER 9

Amy Brandt

Partner, Falfurrias Capital Partners

"I really feel that the kids who are meant to be
yours find you and end up in your family."

I met Amy through a mutual friend who knew straightaway that we would get along. Though it's easy to believe that Amy's professional curriculum vitae is the most impressive part of her, she is impressive in another way too: her love for children who need her.

After graduating from Arizona State University College of Law, her intelligence, quick wit, and perseverance enabled her to rise quickly through the corporate ranks, becoming a chief operating officer by the time she was only twenty-seven. Over the last two decades, Amy has been an accomplished entrepreneur and senior executive, sitting on various corporate boards. Most recently she became the first female partner at her private equity firm. Prior to that she was the president and CEO of First American Docutech and has also been awarded HousingWire's Vanguard Award and the Institute of International Education's Centennial Medal. I told you she's impressive.

Amy's journey as a mother, though, is just as profound. There are so many parts of her life and personality that I relate to, from being raised by younger parents to our work ethic and even the shared experience of buying several pregnancy tests at the drugstore because one wasn't enough. She is a force, and I am thrilled to let her tell her story.

Climbing the Ladder

When I was a kid, I loved riding horses and grew close to my horse trainer. Not only was she a great teacher, but I was intrigued by her family life because she had a household of kids whom she was fostering or had adopted. All of her kids were special, and it was because of her that at a young age I thought that maybe I would adopt someday. But that brief thought of motherhood was really the extent of it. I wasn't one of those girls playing with dolls and dreaming of motherhood; one of my favorite childhood gifts was the briefcase my dad gave to me for my seventh birthday. And yes, I still have it.

When I was born, my dad was playing football at the University of Utah and my mom was working in the medical center there. They were very young. They had started dating in seventh grade, had gotten married when they were nineteen, and had me when they were twenty-one. Once I was coming, my dad left the university, took over his father's business, and became a successful entrepreneur. My parents bought a little ranch to raise their young family. They grew vegetables and raised chickens, and Mom was into health and natural childbirth. She stayed at home and did all the mom things with quite a bit of style. We called her "Mrs. America" because she was always put together well. Dad used to take me to work with him and let me attend his meetings. I looked up to my dad's business skills, especially how he dealt with people. From a young age I knew that I wanted to have a successful career. I was not as drawn to homemaking and children.

I focused on school, studied hard, and attended undergraduate school at the University of Southern California and law school at Arizona State University in rapid succession. After school, I turned my focus to building my career. I started working three jobs while I was still in law school, including clerking for a federal judge. After I began in sales at a financial services business owned by a big private equity fund, I realized how naturally that came to me. I guess Dad taking me to his meetings really helped me hone my sales and negotiation skills.

I got married in my third year of law school, at age twenty-three.

By 1997, even though I had my law degree, I had already become the top salesperson at the financial company and was moving up the ranks quickly. I was focused on driving my career forward, whereas my friends were having kids. Having kids of my own just was not a priority. That would happen someday. My husband, however, did want children and was asking me to give it a try.

Nearly two years after getting married, I thought, "Okay, I'll go off birth control for two months and see what happens." That very much reflects my age. I was oblivious to the process of pregnancy and childbirth, which usually requires more than marking off a few weeks in your daily calendar.

I went off in November and didn't think about it again. In the spring, I was working hard, and I was exhausted. I had never been that tired in my life. One day as I was driving home, I called my mom and said, "I'm so tired. This is not normal."

She said, "Maybe you're pregnant."

I said, "That's not possible."

She said, "Isn't it?"

I pulled over, ran into a drugstore, and bought several pregnancy tests. I went home and took them all—and they all came back positive. I was shocked that it could actually happen so quickly. By the time I went to the doctor, I was already fourteen weeks pregnant. I hadn't realized I was so far along; I had been buried in work.

Of course, I immediately thought, "What am I going to do with my job?"

I was under a lot of pressure, and in those days, it wasn't considered great when you had a baby and were trying to rise in your profession. People immediately assumed that you were going to stay home and, once your pregnancy leave was over, quit your job. So I wasn't excited about telling people at the office. My husband and I were largely relying on my income in sales, and I was doing very well. So I didn't want to lose that.

I called my company and asked about the maternity leave policy. It was pathetic: the company would pay a tiny percentage of my base pay while I took time off, but it didn't compare to the income we depended on. I told the people at the company that I wasn't going to take leave. They informed me that taking a certain amount of time off was mandatory unless I got a doctor's note saying I didn't need time off. So I got one.

I was not going to give up my career, and no one was going to stop me. I was still going to do everything I'd worked toward. I had to have an emergency C-section because the baby was over ten pounds and labor wasn't progressing. Cole was born on a Thursday, and I went back to work on Monday. I chose that then, but I would never recommend it to anyone or do it again.

For all my focus and planning, I couldn't plan how motherhood inevitably changes you. While I was pregnant, I had started wondering what my baby was going to be like. When Cole was born, I was excited to see his little face. For being so sophisticated and put together at work, I definitely was the opposite at home. I couldn't believe this child was mine, and I didn't quite know what to do with him.

Still, I was convinced that I could do it all. Work became increasingly challenging when Cole was young, as I was really rising in the ranks. I breastfed for four months, so I'd pump at work and in the car. I was fortunate that Cole was an easy baby, and I had a really great older nanny who had raised a lot of kids. So somehow, we managed to get through.

A Little Girl

I wasn't eager to get pregnant again because it takes a lot out of you physically, and by then I was president and CEO of the company and had even more responsibilities. But when Cole was around three and a half, I started thinking, "I don't want Cole to be an only child. I want him to have someone to grow up with."

I had a feeling that if I had another baby naturally it would be a son, because there are a lot of boys in the family. I thought, "I wish I could have a daughter." The more I thought about it, the more I knew what to do. So I suggested to my husband, "Let's adopt."

My husband was really worried about potentially having to deal with birth parents down the road. My parents were also trepidatious at first. They said, "We have these biological grandchildren. We're not sure how we're going to feel about this new child. We just don't know." There had not been any adoptions in our family, and I think they were being emotionally honest with me.

But I was determined, and my husband eventually got on board. I looked at both domestic and international options because I really didn't have a preference. I believe that babies are babies and it doesn't matter where they come from. It's heartbreaking that there are children in all parts of the world who need homes, especially countries that lack access to medical care and birth control. I kept reading stories about the huge problem in Guatemala with officials literally finding babies discarded on the streets. Our minds were made up, and we chose to pursue a Guatemalan adoption.

I put my legal background to use to manage the detailed paperwork, including the home study report you had to submit. It took a year to get all the paperwork in order.

Once the home report was complete, I researched adoption agencies to facilitate the international aspect of coordinating with the Guatemalan government. After we chose one, I submitted the paperwork to the government, and not long after, we got the call that we had been accepted to adopt a child.

The agency started sending pictures of available babies. That was honestly the hardest thing about the process; I felt very conflicted about having to choose a child. However, when the agency sent me the picture of a beautiful little girl with big brown eyes born that very day, we said, "That's her." It had become real. The baby had a face (and a name), and we started the last step of the adoption process to bring Alissa home.

I thought the hard part was over and we'd be able to go down to Guatemala and get her within a few months. She would still be an infant when she came to us, so her life wouldn't be disrupted too much.

Unfortunately, just as we were ready to petition the court formally and appear, the Guatemalan government placed a moratorium on all international adoptions. The government was changing the laws, and no one was sure when—or if—the moratorium would be lifted. It was a difficult time, full of uncertainty. We weren't sure what was going to happen or if we would ever get the little girl. Many people suggested that the best path might be to start over and choose another country and baby. But I just couldn't do that. I knew Alissa was waiting for us. So we waited for her.

Thankfully, Alissa had wonderful foster parents, and they sent me pictures and videos along with updates during that seemingly endless period of limbo. We slowly began speaking to our son about the fact that Alissa would be joining our family one day. He was only four at the time, so I am not sure he really got it because he was nonchalant about it, but we kept talking to him about her.

Eleven months later, while I was on a road show taking my company public and working through the transaction details to sell it, I got a call from the agency. The people there told me, "The government has temporarily lifted the adoption moratorium, but there's only a very small window before it closes. You have to come in the next forty-eight hours."

The nursery in our home had been ready and waiting for almost a year, and so had we. It had been hard wondering every day if her crib would ever be slept in or the toys we had purchased ever used. I was so happy to get the call. However, being on a road show meant doing back-to-back meetings, and it was the worst timing ever. But I thought, "It doesn't matter. I have to go." Once again, I knew I wouldn't be able to take official leave from work, because we were in the thick of negotiating the sale of the company. I thought, "At least the baby will be home. Then we'll go from there."

My parents lived right down the street, and I was sure we'd figure it out. I called my mom and dad, and my dad was even more nervous now that the prospect of meeting the new grandchild was suddenly imminent.

I wanted my dad to have the same deep bond with Alissa that he has with his other grandchildren. I asked, "Mom, what should I do?"

Mom said, "You're not going to make the way with him. She will make the way with him herself. Let her form her own relationship with him, and don't put any pressure or fear around it." That was great advice. It was an enduring lesson that you cannot step in and solve every issue; sometimes you need to step back and have faith.

My husband and I went to the airport and got onto the next flight. When we landed in Guatemala, we went to our hotel room, and at 7:00 p.m., there was a knock on the door. When I opened it, the adoption agency representative said hello and a tiny young toddler stood in the hall looking up at me.

Her foster parents did not come due to agency protocol, and they told us that they were very sad to let her go but also very hopeful for her future. They had gone to great lengths to prepare her for that moment, even spending two months of their own salary to buy her a beautiful dress and shoes and other items to present her to us. That was so moving, yet heartbreaking to me, and a reminder of the great responsibility we had to love and care for Alissa.

It was clear that Alissa was attached to them and she was scared. She didn't know us. She was used to her family and her life and didn't know why we were there. She cried quite a bit, and we stayed up that whole first night, trying to comfort her. I felt so bad for her and the shock she was going through and wanted to do anything I could to make her comfortable. I speak passable Spanish, which isn't a perfect cultural tie, but I hoped it would make her feel a bit more at home. Strange people and a strange language together are a lot. I held her and comforted her in Spanish. It was a rough night.

Our court date to finalize the adoption was early the next morning. I was exhausted, but when we got there, I was relieved when Alissa started playing and interacting with another kid sitting next to us who was also waiting for their adoption to close. I was so happy to see her doing better. In just one night, I was already bonded to her and wanted to do everything in the world not just to make her comfortable but to give her the opportunity to thrive. She was a special gift to our family, and I was overwhelmed with gratitude to her mother, who had given us the privilege of raising her, and her foster parents, who had provided her with such a good start.

After court we went to breakfast, and I ordered Alissa oatmeal, thinking that it would be good for her. I was used to my son being a picky eater and wanting only pizza or chicken fingers. Alissa was the opposite: she grabbed my plate and started eating my bacon and eggs. I said, "Look at her go!" It was a nice light moment and so good to laugh after the intensity we had all been through together the last twenty-four hours. We were already becoming a family, and my husband and I got our first glimpse of the confident and assertive person she would become.

When we brought Alissa home, Cole was five. And like most

five-year-olds, he was jealous about having to share his parents' attention with a new sibling. Even though they were quite different—she loved animals and he loved video games—it was clear that he loved her, too.

After Alissa met Cole, it was time for my dad to meet his new granddaughter. He was nervous when he walked in, but both my parents were open and really made the effort. My dad has a mustache, and not every child wants to go to him because they aren't used to facial hair. However, Alissa immediately wanted to go to him, raising her arms up and reaching for him. "Hi, Papa," she said, as if they'd known each other forever. I couldn't believe it. How did she know we call him Papa? How did she know to say hi? She was the first grandbaby who had gone to him before anyone else—and from that moment on, she had his heart. She had my mom's as well. They are both now adoption advocates and tell anyone who says that Alissa is lucky to have us that we are the ones who are lucky to have her in our family. Mom was right: Alissa made her own way!

I continued to speak Spanish with her, but she learned English quickly. Within a couple of months, I'd ask her something in Spanish and she'd answer in English. She also found her way to the horse barn as soon as she could walk and rode her pony every day. I was so proud of her for acclimating and thriving.

Teens in Need

Our family of four charged on for several years as the kids grew and my work continued to be busy. But our family unit didn't last for long. In 2009, after thirteen years of marriage, my husband's and my relationship had been damaged beyond repair due to years of divergent career paths and stressors. We had tried to work things out, but we had become very different people from when we had first been married. It was a very bitter pill to swallow, and I found myself in a state of shock. After all, I had really expected to be like my parents and stay together for a lifetime. It took me a while to accept that was not my path.

After my divorce, I heard that the guy I had dated through-out high school was suffering. His wife had died, and he now had four young kids he was raising on his own: two older boys and two younger girls. Amanda was nearly three, and Shelly was just six months old. My heart broke for those children. Their father and I had kept in touch through the years, so I reached out and told him to come to Texas so I could help them. I helped get them into a house, and he and I subsequently started dating again, eventually moving in together. I was happy to help with the kids and especially connected with the girls because they were younger and needed a lot. They were too little to remember their mother, and I was all they knew. My kids loved having them around, and they formed a little kid pack. Cole always carried Shelly around, and Alissa immediately assumed the big-sister role. Even after my relationship with their father foundered, I maintained my relationship with the kids.

However, one day when the girls were seven and nine years old, their father decided to pick up and move them all. All too suddenly they were gone, and I was unable to find or contact them. I kept leaving messages that went unanswered. I was panicked and started trying to reach his family members to get information. I finally heard from one of his relatives what had happened. He had abruptly left town with all four kids and moved to a commune in another city across the country. A veteran of the army, he wanted to retreat from society. I was relieved to finally know where they were, but it was not a place that allowed me to communicate with them and I had concerns about it.

I had no parental rights. There was nothing I could do except wait and hope that they would reach out to me one day.

I'm a problem solver, so it was really hard to not be able to solve that problem. I kept wondering if the kids were okay. I reached out to him several times and always left the same message: "If you want me to take the kids or provide any assistance, call me."

But for years I didn't hear a word and never knew if the kids were okay. It was devastating not to be able to do anything. Alissa was upset, and so was Cole. Alissa said, "Don't ever marry anyone with kids. I don't want to have to go through losing sisters ever again." I obviously could not make that promise, but I understood where she was coming from.

Several years later, one day out of the blue, he called and said, "I want to leave this place immediately." I didn't ask a lot of questions. I was just happy that they were okay. So I helped them move to a better place, and I started taking the girls regularly again.

By that time, I had remarried, and we had moved from Texas to Arizona. My husband is a twenty-year army veteran, a really wonderful person, and though he never had his own children, he is very good with them. I had unintentionally fulfilled Alissa's request to marry someone with no children. One day, about two years after I was in contact with the kids again, the girls called. They wanted to live with me full-time.

Their father again wanted to retreat from society. The girls did not like the commune they had lived in and did not want to go back. There were a lot of factors in play, but that was a crisis for the kids. I would do anything for the girls, and the years they had been gone had left a hole in my heart. So I said, "Of course."

I was not sure how my husband would react; it's a big ask to take in two more children, especially those of an ex-boyfriend. But I really felt it was the only choice to make and hoped he would agree. I wanted them to feel loved and accepted and to be able to thrive in their new home.

He knew that I had always felt like their mother and had been distraught during the years they had been gone. He had also gotten to know them, as we had been taking them during summers and holidays since they had left the commune. He immediately and without question said, "Yes."

I was thrilled with his lack of hesitation and the strength of his commitment. Raising children is never easy, and I was happy that we would approach it in such a unified fashion.

I called their father and said, "I want to come get the girls; can I bring them here?"

I was devastated when he said, "No. I'm going to move them with me." Based on that conversation, it was clear that the girls were right; he was having a crisis. He stated that where they were moving, they would not have access to technology and would no longer be able to visit or have any communication with us.

The thought of the girls disappearing again scared me, and although I wanted to go pick them up, I knew that was not legally possible. So I did the only thing I could do: I prayed. I pleaded, "God, if they're meant to be with me, then intervene. Do something."

The next morning, to my surprise, their father called me and said, "If you're going to take them, that's fine, I'll sign the custody papers. But you have to take them in the next few days or not at all." Ultimately, he wanted to do the best thing for them, but it was very hard.

As fate would have it, I was on the road again. That time, however, it wasn't for business. I was on my way to a riding competition with Alissa, who shows horses all around the country and is an accomplished jumper. But again, even though it was challenging timing, it didn't matter; there was only one thing to do. We had to make sure that the girls made it to us safely. I told both of my kids I was going to bring the girls to our house and that I would officially make them part of our family.

My next call was to my lawyers, who drew up papers immediately. I signed them and sent them overnight to their father. As promised, he signed and returned them promptly. The nearest airport between us at the time was in Las Vegas, and on my way to the horse show, I picked them up.

When I arrived at the airport to pick up the girls, who were now twelve and fourteen, it was a bittersweet moment. I was so excited to see them, and they were happy to be there. They were also conflicted about leaving their father and scared about all the changes. Because they had left so quickly, they had not been able to bring much with them.

The girls had been through a lot in their short lives, starting very early with the death of their mother. Nothing could change that, but we had to focus on healing, growth, and all the possibilities for the future. I told them, "Life is what you make it. You're in charge of it. You don't have to let the things that happened to you define you. You get to define what you are and what your life is going to be. You're in charge of that. I can help you; I can provide you resources and support, but you own that journey."

The girls saw a wonderful therapist, and I really try not to be overly intrusive about it. They own it and manage it the way they want to. I feel that therapy and owning their journey has helped them make incredible progress. Cole and Alissa picked up right where they left off with the girls. My son, now out of college and working in another city, still talks to them and visits them regularly. Alissa loves them, too, and has jumped right back into the big-sister role. The girls' older brothers are marines, and we love it when they visit, too. They are part of the family. It was a lot for all of us to go through and we've had some ups and downs, but overall, they're doing well, and I'm very proud of them. Amanda just graduated from high school and is attending college—which she loves so far. It is close to home, and she is helping with driving her sister to high school. Shelly is into track, wants to get a scholarship, and has the best sense of humor that always keeps us laughing. I'm proud of the strides they've made and the grown-ups they are becoming.

Every child you have is unique, whether they are biologically yours or adopted, and you build a relationship with each one individually. So even if you don't have those months while they're in your belly to build a relationship, once you have them, you start from there and create it.

An Oscar for Best Mom

Motherhood comes in all shapes and sizes, but one thing persists across all realms of it: it's hard! And for me, it was really hard being a working mom. You have so much mom guilt: What's going to happen when I'm not there? Will my kids think differently of me because I spend so much time working? I spent too many days, hopefully away from their eyes, being worried about that and thinking I wasn't a mom like my mom had been; she had been on every field trip, at PTA meetings, and at the school bus stop morning and afternoon and had packed my lunch every day.

I wasn't like that. I didn't like PTA meetings. I didn't do the mom things. But that didn't mean they didn't get done. It just wasn't always me doing them.

It wasn't until my son went off to college that I knew the answer to my worries and self-doubt. He called me and said, "I feel so much more adjusted than a lot of these kids. Some are drinking and partying and acting like idiots because they're away from their mom for the first time. I'm fine and I miss you, but I'm not losing my mind like some of these other kids, and I want to thank you for how you raised me. I'm so much more capable than a lot of people around me."

My kids still call me every day and want to take all their vacations with us; they still want to be around us and hang out at the house on weekends. I wish I had gotten rid of all the mom guilt earlier. I wish I'd known then that I could embrace doing things my way and they'd be okay.

My husband threw a surprise party for my fiftieth birthday, and it was Oscar themed. It was great because my kids gave beautiful speeches and different awards they'd made for me. They were so proud of the things that I've accomplished and done. It was nice to hear them say, "We have a mom who's different from everyone else's mom, and we love her" and to know they're super proud of that. Don't get me wrong, they still have their moments, but that's a part of being a mom. I love that I have a good relationship with each of my children and I'm glad I became a mom after all.

Some women start planning their pregnancy the minute they are ready. For me, having a child wasn't at the top of my priority list. It's almost as though I tried to avoid being a mother, because I kept putting off getting pregnant and I really didn't enjoy being pregnant once I was. I'm sure a lot of women feel that way but are afraid to say it out loud. It's okay. In spite of that, there's no doubt that I was meant to be a mother. And I really feel that the kids who are meant to be yours find you and end up in your family. There's no difference between the ones who come to you biologically and the ones who come to you other ways. I was meant to have these children. They found me.

And I love being their mom.

CHAPTER 10

Marion Champlain

FOX Viewer; Owner, Marion's Hospitality
From her daughter, Sandra Champlain

"Work hard, play hard."

As a country music fan, I have always loved the band Rascal Flatts. But it wasn't until I heard the story of Marion Champlain that I really understood the meaning of the song "Fast Cars and Freedom." When FOX asked viewers to write in about their moms, Sandra Champlain wrote about her mom, Marion. I was excited to hear about how she had made bold choices to rediscover herself and her love of car races. Marion is fearless and loves adventure. Not following the traditional path of motherhood, Marion decided to re-create herself after her kids were born to follow her passion for adventure and became an icon in the race car industry.

Here is her story, as told by her daughter Sandra.

A Go-Getter

My mom is so extraordinary. She's eighty-one and is a beautiful soul who has helped so many people. She is as wise as they come and has always been a go-getter. Being her child with that kind of positive attitude empowering me has been wonderful. Her best advice has always been, "You can make anything happen, and if you go for it, and fail, so what? Just try something else." That's who she is.

My mom was born on April 18, 1942, during World War II in Hamburg, Germany. Her mother was American and her father German. Since her father spoke English, when war hit, he was drafted into the German Army as a translator and went off to fight at the Russian front, while my mom, along with her siblings, lived with their mom and grandmother. In July 1943, Hamburg was bombed over the course of seven days, and forty thousand civilians died. My mom and her family were lucky to survive, but it was terrifying. She tells the story that when she was just three, she remembers that her mother disappeared one day while she was out looking for food, which was scarce, for the family. The police detained her, believing she might be a spy, and grilled her for details about her family in the United States and her husband. They finally let her go a couple of weeks later, and she returned home.

In the months after the war ended in 1945, most Americans were forced to leave Germany. In 1946, when my mom was four, they left her father behind in Germany and traveled to the United States via ship, first landing in New York, then traveling to Minnesota to stay with her mom's family. It was two years before Germans were allowed into the United States, and once they were, her father was one of the first German soldiers allowed to enter. Once the family was reunited, they built their life in the very small town of Carlton, Minnesota.

Mom tells the story that on her first day of kindergarten in Minnesota, the teacher tied a ribbon around her head to keep her jaw shut because English was the only language to be spoken. Many Americans disliked Germans and did not want to hear their language. But my mom is such a survivor. Not knowing the language or landscape didn't deter her from being a bubbly, friendly little girl who quickly learned to speak English. She was very popular all throughout her schooling, and not only was the head cheerleader but went to nine proms! She decided early on to follow her mantra: work hard, play hard. In 1953, her younger brother, Bobby, was born.

In 1960, right after Mom graduated from high school, she went into the air force because she was patriotic, she knew she would earn a living and would have her room and board paid for, and she loved the idea of traveling. She did basic training at Lackland Air Force Base in San Antonio, Texas. The new recruits were given an aptitude test at the completion of her training, and only four out of the eighty-four in her class "went into the sky" as flight attendants. She was thrilled. She went to McGuire Air Force Base in New Jersey and flew on DC-6 military passenger aircraft to Europe and many other places, meeting various people. She once had Charles Lindbergh as a passenger on a flight. What a thrill that must have been. But my favorite story she recalls during this time in her life is from when she went to France for the first time and went to a cabaret.

As she walked inside, someone said, "Would you like a cock-tail?"

She earnestly replied, "Shrimp, please."

I am sure the waiter looked at her as though she was crazy, but up until that point, she had never heard the word "cocktail" in reference to alcohol; she really hadn't been introduced to alcohol at all during her upbringing in small-town Minnesota.

Mom loved her new life, which was full of traveling the world. Tragically, two years into her air force career, she got word that her mother had been killed in an auto accident when her car was hit by a drunk driver. Seat belts didn't exist in most cars at that time. Mom had planned on having a career in the air force and traveling the world, a life of adventure—but in the back seat of the car had been her little brother, Bobby, who was only nine years old. Although he had survived, he was traumatized, and so, at the age of twenty, Mom came home, gave up the air force, and helped her father raise her little brother.

By then she had already met my dad, who was a pilot from Massachusetts. They had met at McGuire Air Force Base. Funny enough, Mom went out with his roommate first, only to realize she liked my dad more. They continued a long-distance relationship and got married on April 4, 1964, in Minnesota. They lived at Tyndall Air Force Base in Florida, where Dad was stationed, and Bobby lived there with them. A year later, they had twins, Heidi and Steve, and in 1966, I came along. Five years later, my younger sister, Karen, was born. My dad traveled a lot for the air force, and there were long periods of time when Mom was left alone to care for Bobby along with her own three children. A few years later, my dad left the service and became a pilot for a commercial airline, so they moved to New England and eventually built their dream house in Connecticut. It was clear that the travel bug never left

Mom, because our family traveled as much as we could. During school vacations, we were always going somewhere new for an adventure.

Reinventing Marion

In 1983, when I was seventeen, my mother and father divorced. My older siblings had a few months of high school left and chose to live with a friend's family close to the high school. My parents ended up selling the house, and my younger sister and I went to live with our dad. I was really close to my dad, and I think that, like my siblings, I didn't really understand what was behind my parents' split. I visited my mom often but was not as close to her as I was to my dad around the time of the divorce.

In 1985, I went off to college and Dad moved to Daytona Beach, Florida, and my younger sister, Karen, moved with him. I stayed there during school breaks and for a year after college. Many times, Mom flew down and visited us. She and my dad remained friendly, and I knew they cared deeply about each other.

Mom opened a small consignment shop called Second Time Around and, after selling it, went to work as a travel agent. But it wasn't all work and no play. It was around that time that Mom started attending auto races at Lime Rock Park in Connecticut with our neighbor and fell in love with the entire experience. She soon became the travel agent for Dyson Racing in Poughkeepsie, New York, and opened her own agency, Kent Travel Center, in 1989.

She made sandwiches for the racing team and even found herself out on the track helping the racers. There is a position on a pit crew known as the "dead man." When a pit stop happens, picture the guy jumping over a pit wall and putting gas into the car with a hose. There's a person actually underneath the gas bin who pulls the trigger; that's the dead man. My mother would put on a helmet and race suit, get under the gas bin, and act as the dead man. She did that year after year.

It wasn't until years later, over a bottle of wine with my mom, as I was trying to figure out what next to do with my own life, that I saw her life from *her* perspective. I realized that as a young woman, she had never really figured out who she was as an individual because her air force career had been cut short to care for her younger brother. Her dreams had always been to explore and travel, and being a stay-at-home mother to four kids had left something missing inside her. She was searching for her identity outside of being a mom and wanted to reinvent herself while she still had time, plus my dad wasn't always easy to be with. For some people, it may be hard to wrap their mind around walking away from a marriage and home because something feels lacking, but she wanted to find happiness in herself and not just in her role as a mother.

After that heart-to-heart conversation with her, following years of uncertainty, I learned what a lovely human being she really is, and it was the first time I thought, "I need to see life from someone else's perspective instead of judging their decisions and assuming they are wrong."

It was during that same conversation that my life changed. I am a chef by trade, and at the time I was also searching for my life's purpose. My mom listened to me as I had listened to her. In culinary school I had always excelled in desserts and chocolates. She told me that when she had been a flight attendant in the air force, flying across the Atlantic, her favorite thing to do was to have coffee and a Hershey's bar. There was nothing better in the world.

She said, "You make such wonderful chocolates. Move in with

me, and start a coffee and chocolate store. In the winter months when no tourists are around, there are still lots of holidays that are perfect for chocolate gifts, like Christmas and Valentine's Day, and then there's Easter."

That was when Kent Coffee & Chocolate was born, and it existed in Connecticut for thirty years until it was sold to new owners in 2023. Without her insight, I would never have had a successful shop that brought treats into thousands of homes.

Let's Go to the Races

In Daytona, there's an annual endurance race in which three different drivers race for a team and their cars go around the track for twenty-four hours to see whose team has the most stamina. In 1987, without asking me, my mom volunteered me to cook for the Dyson team, figuring that I would help, having graduated from the Culinary Institute of America. She told them, "My daughter's a chef, these guys need to eat properly."

How could I say no to my mother? And an adventure? So we rented a little motor home, and out of it I'd pump out meals and she'd deliver them to the pit. At that time, I was cooking for just the one race team, and she was making travel arrangements (and sandwiches), and we'd do only the big twelve- and twenty-four-hour races a couple of times a year.

Then not long after, at the local Lime Rock racetrack, the actor Craig T. Nelson, known for the television series *Coach*, was driving a race car and sharing a hospitality setup with Rob Dyson's team. I went as a guest, and although the food looked beautiful, it wasn't great. When I found out how much they were spending,

I thought, "There's a better way to do this." The race cars go well over two hundred miles per hour. The guys work really hard with those cars, so we wanted to feed them a nutritious meal and also create an atmosphere of a home away from home. They needed quality.

I said, "You know, we could do this." And Mom agreed. Craig T. Nelson and Rob Dyson agreed as well and decided to give us the opportunity. In mid-1996, we started Marion's Hospitality full-time, going to every race. At first we had a small tent that held maybe forty to fifty team members, together with some guests and sponsors. Then eventually someone from another team would ask who we were, and then we'd have another team in the tent. At a race in Atlanta, Paul Newman walked into the tent with Don Panoz, the creator of the nicotine patch and also the man behind the revival of the Road Atlanta racecourse. After they ate, they said, "We like what you do." And the tent got even bigger. Sometimes my mom even coordinated Paul Newman's travel.

My mom is very humble; she just did her job, treated everyone like real people, and took care of them. She saw it as fulfilling a need. The British race car driver James Weaver said in an interview, "In such a dangerous sport, Marion provides a place of comfort, great food and a warm family environment while we are away from home."

Wherever we were in the United States and Canada, every tent was created to give the sense of comfort and home. We fashioned a fun atmosphere with music playing, great conversation, and terrific food. Two hours before anyone got into a race car, we had coffee on and a big breakfast buffet. All the meals were buffets so people could come and go all day long. And even when they stopped racing in the evening, we'd stay open an hour or two after that so no one would go to bed hungry. You name it, we had it.

We also had snacks galore. My mom is fondly remembered by the race teams as driving down pit lane in a golf cart hauling a cooler filled with ice cream bars. She even gave them out to teams we weren't contracted to feed, but that's just who she is. As she grew older, she started slowing down a bit, so I gave out the ice cream while she drove the golf cart.

Of course, we grew out of the mobile home and eventually had a big white SUV pulling a sixteen-foot trailer. When we got to a race-track, we'd plug in the trailer, and it became our walk-in refrigerator. Then we grew even more to have a thirty-foot box truck. We'd usually hire a truck driver from one of the races, and we traveled all over California, Atlanta, Wisconsin, Connecticut, Ohio, Florida, and so many more places. Although we always hired someone from the track to drive our big truck, one time we ran into a problem and my mom had to drive it herself into Canada. But she didn't flinch; she had no fear. She just said, "Things have to happen, and so we have to make them happen." And she hopped right in and drove that monster herself.

Some of our largest single meals were served to 1,500 people. Mom had a table right by the entrance of the tent with her spreadsheet, and she'd mark off which team each person was on. She always remembered everyone's name. She was also tough when she needed to be. If you didn't belong in our tent—non–racing people were always trying to sneak in—she'd show you the door. It was common for big race team owners and drivers such as Roger Penske, Jim France, and Chip Ganassi to sit with her at her table. Mom's a brilliant woman, and they had amazing conversations. So many things happened at her table.

A race car driver would sit and say, "Marion, I don't have a ride for the next race."

And Mom would say, "Leave it with me."

Then one of the team owners would sit down, and she'd say, "Do you know this guy? I think you should give him a chance." And the driver would get another ride.

Whatever anyone needed, even if it was a part for a car, they'd no doubt find someone who could help under our tent. So whether it was a crew member, a truck driver, or a race car driver, Mom helped connect all of them. In time, our tent even became a good-luck charm; if you ate under our tent, you ended up in the winner's circle. One year, at one of the Daytona races, the top ten winners were all from teams we had fed.

At one of the year-end banquets—we were always invited as part of the team—during a slide show of various racing cars, a picture flashed up of my mother in her golf cart delivering ice cream and the whole place cheered. At another one, one of the people who ran the series said, "An army marches on its stomach, and thank goodness we have Marion Champlain." The room exploded with clapping and cheering; she got a standing ovation. They really did love her.

Grief

Though Marion's Hospitality was successful, I had to face the fact that my father was dying of cancer. I was sad, and my mom was there for me—and him. In 2010, when he was in a care facility, my mom and I went to see him; it was on the same day as their wedding anniversary, April 4. It was also Easter Sunday, and Mom took Dad an Easter meal and we spent the day together. That last day they were together, they got to say their goodbyes and express their love for each other after being through so much together. He passed away the next month, and I will never forget that beautiful moment they shared. It brought some comfort.

We all know what grief for losing a loved one is like, and I grieved. It was a big loss, and again my mom was there for me. When Dad died, it set me searching, and I found out how our brain chemistry and perception changes when we grieve. I studied evidence of the afterlife and shared what I'd learned, publishing a book titled *We Don't Die: A Skeptic's Discovery of Life After Death*. I could not have processed my grief and produced a book had my mother not encouraged me to reach for more, to try something new, to push forward.

We had no idea that in March 2020 we would be hit with another kind of grief. A few days after purchasing $50,000 worth of food and setting up our hospitality tent for a race in Sebring, Florida, the race was canceled because of covid-19. The world shut down, literally. All the upcoming races were canceled.

We returned the food we could and donated the rest of it to local shelters and churches. We packed up all our equipment and stored it. We went home to Rhode Island, parked our thirty-foot box truck, and sat down to deal with the uncertainty. We always thought the pause would be temporary.

Once the races began again, they allowed only single-serve to-go meals, and people couldn't congregate together under one tent. We really fought it; we thought that somehow, some way, we could save our business. But the race teams got used to takeout while others just loaded up on snacks. The desire to have the large tent and buffet had dwindled with lingering pandemic skepticism about people being close to one another. It was starting to feel like we weren't going to go back.

After we made the call to close the business, we parked our big box truck in front of the house and started selling off equipment. We still have a basement full of pots, pans, ladles, and many other things that remain up for grabs.

Another New Beginning

It was tough saying goodbye to our business; it had been a big part of our life, and we were sad. But fate had a different plan. Our time to grieve for my father and the closure of our business was cut short when Mom found a lump on her breast a year into the pandemic. She was diagnosed with breast cancer after getting a biopsy. Fortunately, because she found it early, it was stage 1, and after a lumpectomy, she recovered quickly. That was a big wake-up call for both of us. I was in my midfifties, she was in her late seventies; neither of us was getting any younger. Did we really want to be on the road all year long feeding people? As much as we had enjoyed the work, it came with long, eighteen-hour days, and we got very little sleep. It was as though the business closed at the perfect time because we needed to stay local during her cancer treatments anyway. So we ended up leaving racing while we were at the top of our game.

Mom also decided that it was time for a new house. She sure does like adventures. She found a house she liked in Tiverton, Rhode Island, half an hour from Newport. It's in the woods, filled with windows. Birds, squirrels, deer, and even wild turkeys frequent the yard. The quality of life we have now is really wonderful, and we realized it was time to move on. Covid just gave us the push to be where we needed to be.

She's the strongest woman I know. Her advice to me has always been, "Sandra, don't wait for things to happen; make them happen." She'll even tell you that very rarely do you need to give someone advice. Just listen to them, and they will figure out what's right on their own.

This morning, she said to me, "Nobody knows how long we are on Earth."

She is so right.

We have created a blissful routine. Every morning I brew the coffee and we watch the gang on *FOX & Friends*. She has FOX on all day. She lets me know what's happening in the world.

We appreciate life and each other. I am blessed to be able to spend so much time with my mom. Every day I find something else new about her through the random stories she tells when something comes on TV that reminds her of one of her escapades. Recently a cooking show came on about pie, and she nonchalantly asked, "Did I ever tell you about those ladies and the peach pies?"

I said, "No, what happened?"

She continued, "It was years ago. There were some women who had obviously come from a bake shop, because they had tons of peach pies. But their car had flipped over. I drove by and it was in the middle of nowhere, so I knew I had to get them out of the car." My mother just reached in and pulled those ladies out of the vehicle.

Another day she told me that once she had been scuba diving on the island of Bonaire in the Caribbean. She was on the dock when she heard someone screaming. It turned out that a blind man had gone for a swim; he had become disorientated and was crying out for help. My mom dived in and saved him.

She has enough stories to fill a library.

Mom doesn't see herself as anything important. But I know—and everyone who meets her knows, too—that she is a uniquely intuitive, insightful, caring, generous, loving person. She's amazing, and she is my best friend.

The racing world agrees. On her eightieth birthday, race car drivers and friends from all over made a video to wish her a happy birthday. Hélio Castroneves, a racer and *Dancing with the Stars* alum, said it best: "Marion, we love you! We miss you!"

I know she misses them, too.

I never cease to be amazed by my mom, and I tell her so. But she wonders what all the hoopla is about and says, "You've got to do what you've got to do. You have to get in there if no one else is going to help."

PART IV

Valor

Courage takes many forms. Those in the military sacrifice so much for their country and for every one of us. They lay down their lives for our freedom—a sacrifice that is unparalleled. But the hardships of war reach much further than the soldiers. Their families, their friends, and the journalists who put themselves in harm's way to document conflicts around the globe—and their loved ones—also pay a price.

Some scars are visible; others are hidden beneath the surface. And the courage displayed on and off the battle-field by all those touched by war doesn't end once the battle is over.

CHAPTER 11

Jennifer Griffin

Chief National Security Correspondent, FOX News

"I believe that being a mother
in the Middle East was a key part of my
achieving success as a journalist."

I am in awe of Jennifer Griffin. She is an action hero mom who has reported on military conflicts for FOX News for almost three decades, living and working in war zones from Jerusalem to Moscow. Jennifer's grit and stamina in difficult war situations are matched by her courage battling breast cancer, diagnosed soon after delivering her child. She's a force of nature.

The day I interviewed Jennifer for this book, she was at the Pentagon chasing down a story about an assassination attempt at the Kremlin during the second year of the Ukraine war. I asked her to talk about her motherhood journey coexisting with unrelenting national security responsibilities. She was gracious enough to share her remarkable story and her precious time—interrupted by simultaneous calls from General Laura Richardson's aide from the US Southern Command and from her sick son, who wanted her to bring home ice cream. She juggled us all effortlessly.

Go to the Ends of the Earth for Your Dreams

From the very beginning, my mother, Carolyn, told my sisters and me to go to the ends of the earth for our dreams; it was advice I took very literally. During my sophomore year studying journalism at Harvard, I decided to go to South Africa, as apartheid was coming to an end, and intern for a local newspaper in Soweto.

My mother is the founder of MetroStage, a nonprofit theater company in Alexandria, Virginia, where I grew up. She has always been politically active and very involved in what's going on in the world through art and her theater productions. On her stage, she produces cutting-edge political theater and, at that time, plays by Athol Fugard. Regarded as South Africa's greatest playwright, Fugard was doing a lot of antiapartheid plays at the Market Theatre in Johannesburg and became known more widely later for the 2005 Oscar-winning film of his novel *Tsotsi*.

When I left for Johannesburg, my mother told me to make sure I went to the Market Theatre. And because I always do what my mother says, not long after I arrived, I sought out the venue. Thanks to my mother's recommendation, I met an amazing South African playwright—and subsequently, my mother brought his play to Alexandria for a US premiere.

My mother's embrace of world culture is why she innately understands why I do what I do in my profession. From the beginning she supported me—even when I wheedled my way into Archbishop Desmond Tutu's backyard for Nelson and Winnie Mandela's first press conference, the day after Nelson Mandela was released from prison on February 11, 1990. All the greats, including Ted Koppel and other top television anchors, were at that press conference. My mother thought it was funny that even though I was by no means an accredited journalist at that point, I used my Harvard student ID to talk my way in.

Following my mother's advice to follow my dreams led me to something else in South Africa: an AP reporter, Greg Myre, the man who would become my partner for life and the reason I became a mom.

Mogadishu

After I graduated from college in 1992, I made my way to Mogadishu, Somalia, where Greg was covering the famine, first flying into Nairobi, Kenya, from South Africa. I then began negotiating my way onto a small-plane flight into Mogadishu, as no commercial flights could fly there because of all the shooting in the capital. As I was trying to negotiate with the khat dealers at one end of the airport to pay my weight in khat and fly into Mogadishu with them, a Canadian journalist secured a spot on a UNICEF plane for me instead.

When I arrived, I found Greg staying at the UNICEF House. He was surprised to see me, but we didn't miss a beat; we worked side by side from that moment forward, traveling the world together. Our next assignment took us to Islamabad, Pakistan, where, in 1994, we decided to get married; we spent our honeymoon in Kabul, Afghanistan, at the time when the Taliban was being formed.

We traveled to places such as Saddam Hussein's Iraq, Syria, Iran, Lebanon, Somalia, Pakistan, and Afghanistan, covering many stories. At that time there were no cell phones; it was not like the modern day, and we were not modern journalists. We disappeared for weeks and months at a time when covering dangerous areas with no way of communicating with the outside world. We were having amazing adventures, living on the edge, sometimes finding ourselves in danger, and loving every assignment and every story.

I wasn't a mother yet, and there was no way a child would fit into that lifestyle. We figured we would get to that. One day the timing would be right. Or so we thought.

From Mogadishu to Motherhood

In 1999, after three intense freelance years in Moscow covering the Kosovo conflict, a news organization, FOX, offered me a full-time job and an assignment covering Jerusalem and the Oslo Peace Talks. Greg and I were exhausted after eight years of wars and decided that moving to Jerusalem would be a chance to leave behind the war zone coverage we'd lived with and start a family. There had never been a more perfect time to begin a new chapter of our life. We headed to Jerusalem thinking our work was going to be easy, maybe even boring. But we were ready to become parents. We both had always wanted that.

Twelve months after moving to Jerusalem—a year before 9/11—I was pregnant with our first daughter, Annalise, and looking forward to meeting my little girl. I got the nursery ready, enjoying the reprieve from the chaos of war, and even found that covering peace was not as boring as I had anticipated. But that wouldn't last. In the fall, shortly after I found out I was pregnant, the Intifada—the Palestinian uprising against the Israeli occupation of the West Bank and Gaza Strip—broke out.

As the stones began flying, I started reporting, despite my morning sickness, and wearing a flak jacket, which fortunately was expandable, as I was expanding by the day. I was often light-headed and hunched over between live shots or looking for a place to throw up.

Throughout the rest of my pregnancy, I covered suicide bombings and military incursions into the West Bank and Gaza, wearing that flak jacket literally up until the day before I gave birth on April 7, 2001, to my first baby. On April 6, I had climbed over a military barricade to enter Ramallah in order to get an interview.

After I got back to Jerusalem that night, my water broke, and we went to Hadassah University Hospital on Mount Scopus. My delivery room had the most beautiful plate glass window with a gorgeous view overlooking the old city of Jerusalem. The anticipation was over; I finally got to look down into my little girl's eyes.

We continued living in Jerusalem, raising Annalise, and it was like nothing I'd ever experienced to watch her grow; everything she did seemed like a revelation. Although I was on a different continent from my mother, I had Rose, a wonderful live-in nanny, I'd met through a diplomat I knew there.

And then everything changed. Five months after Annalise was born, the attack on the World Trade Center in New York City on September 11, 2001, sent shock waves throughout the world—and through our newfound parenthood.

Greg was asked to return to Afghanistan and was one of the first reporters to get in, first going to Kabul. Meanwhile, I was trying to figure out how I could report on it, too; maybe I could take Annalise and our nanny back to Islamabad, where I knew I could leave Annalise safely with friends because we'd lived there a few years. I was torn. How could I miss reporting on that incredible story? But I ultimately opted to stay in Jerusalem.

We decided to add to our family. We had learned that there was never a perfect time to do it. If you wait for the perfect time, you might miss your chance. So when Annalise was a little over a year and a half old, that December I gave birth to my second daughter, Amelia, in the same delivery room where Annalise had made her entrance.

It was just a month or so before the US invasion of Iraq, and at the time, the government was worried that Saddam would fire SCUD missiles, which carried chemical weapons, into Israel. Because of the danger, we were required by law to carry a gas mask on our shoulder that looked like a big purse.

Instead of receiving a box of diapers or formula when I was discharged, the hospital gave me a gas mask tent for Amelia's crib. We were also required by law to have a safe room in our house, a bomb shelter we could seal off completely where the child would be safe if a chemical weapon was fired at Israel.

So that was Amelia's dramatic introduction to this world. Even then my mother supported me, never pressuring me to stop being a reporter or to leave Jerusalem, where we had made our home for years.

Pump in Style

Over the next couple of years, while I was still nursing both daughters, I continued going back and forth to the Gaza Strip. Sometimes I'd be there overnight. I'd carry my Medela breast milk pump with me, which caused a great deal of consternation when my bags were searched at interviews with Hamas leaders because they thought it looked a little like a bomb.

There were other times I'd have no place to store my milk except at the border crossing with young Israeli soldiers who were nice enough to put it into their refrigerator. It was an unconventional upbringing for my daughters.

It's not surprising that one day when Annalise, who was three or four, and her best friend, Benny, the son of a *Washington Post* correspondent, were role playing in the Wohl Rose Park, I heard one of them say, while pretending to hold a phone, "There's been a bombing."

The other one responded, "Have you sent a photographer?"

Clearly my line of work was known in the household.

I had watched my mother produce and run a theater and be a mother without choosing between the two. I had never considered having to choose; I didn't think I had to make a choice. Still, that didn't mean I wouldn't miss some moments along the way once my daughters were no longer infants, when I had to leave to cover a story.

In 2004, when the girls were two and three, my mother and sisters flew to Jerusalem for Christmas. We were doing all the usual sights, planning a wonderful Christmas Eve trip to Bethlehem. To get there, we of course had to go through an Israeli checkpoint on Christmas Eve.

I remember my little girls asking me, "Did the Wise Men have to go this way?"

Once we got there, Bethlehem was beautiful and memorable for the whole family. But elsewhere, tragedy would strike. A massive 9.3 magnitude earthquake struck off the west coast of northern Sumatra, Indonesia, triggering a deadly tsunami that devastated Thailand and Indonesia, claiming more than twenty-five thousand lives.

I got the call to pack my bags and cover the crushing natural disaster before we even had breakfast. I started crying because I didn't want to leave my girls a day after Christmas. But I knew I had to get there as soon as I could. My mom stayed and took care of my girls for the next two weeks. I was fortunate so many times like that, when my mom was my right hand in all things and able to take over.

The Deadliest Battle

In 2007, I was assigned to the Pentagon because we had lived overseas and I had a working knowledge of all the conflict zones where the United States was operating. So we moved back to the States and settled close to DC. I'd loved being overseas, but it was nice to be near my mother and sisters again. A year later, Luke, our youngest, came along, and although he was a surprise, we were thrilled. A boy was another wonderful addition to our family. He was born in March 2009, and per normal, I was nursing and pumping and reporting. Life was good.

Then I faced a battle far more dangerous than any front line I had visited. After escaping injury through all the war zones and death I'd reported on, I had no idea that my life was now in real jeopardy.

One day as I was weaning my infant Luke off nursing, I felt a large lump in the right side of my breast. It had been masked during breast-feeding, when my breasts had been engorged, and now it was the size of a grapefruit. I immediately went to the doctor, and they did a biopsy.

When my doctor told me I had Stage 3 triple-negative breast cancer, I was stunned.

I had been very diligent about my breast health and mammograms because I had breast cancer in my family. I didn't have a known genetic mutation like BRCA 1/2, but I did have a family history and so was vigilant. Because of the pregnancy and breastfeeding, I'd fallen behind with my mammograms a couple of years. I was shocked to find out that not only can you get breast cancer while you're pregnant and nursing, but if you do, it tends to be a more aggressive form.

I was diagnosed on a Friday, and the next Tuesday began seventeen rounds of chemotherapy, followed by a double mastectomy and seven weeks of radiation. Lukey was only six months old as it all began. I tear up now even thinking about it. What a tiny young thing he was, and my girls, too. I had never been afraid during all the time living on the edge, traveling the world alone or with my husband. In all those conflict zones I had worked well on the adrenaline and pressure that come with breaking stories in difficult places.

But I was terrified when faced with the thought that I wouldn't be there for my kids if cancer had its way. I didn't think about the stories I'd miss being at the center of breaking headlines. For the first time in my life, I wasn't torn. I wasn't thinking as a reporter; my focus was solely as a mom. I thought about fighting the awful disease only so I could see my kids grow up. Every maternal instinct I had clicked in, and I fought the cancer as if it were a monster grabbing my children from my arms.

They say it takes a village to raise kids, and I was glad to have mine. At nine and seven, Annalise and Amelia were brave, rock star sisters helping with their baby brother. Our wonderful nanny, Rose, had become a big part of our family and was still with us. My husband, who is as solid as the Rock of Gibraltar, my mom and two sisters, and friends who organized food deliveries, all were in my corner. I was fortunate to have so much support during the fight for my life, not to mention extraordinary support from all my bosses and colleagues at FOX; the company gave me a year off to be treated, get healthy, and be with my family. I'm eternally grateful and loyal to the FOX executives for their extreme compassion during that harrowing time.

Twelve months later, in September 2010, I was cancer free. I was overjoyed, and we celebrated as a family. Then life resumed and I went back to work, flying to Kabul to report on David Petraeus, the general who had just taken over command in Afghanistan.

When I went on air that night for a live shot from a Kabul rooftop, I was overcome with emotion, and I burst into tears. But I managed to collect myself and delivered my report.

It had been such an intense journey, from finding out I had cancer and wondering if I'd be around for my children to coming full circle to healing, knowing that I'd still be able to love and protect them and see them flourish. There's nothing more important to me.

So, ladies, I'm here to advise you: please get your mammograms.

The Mother of All Bow Ties

Sometimes people say to my kids, "Wasn't that irresponsible of your mother?" regarding their childhood overseas. Their general reaction is defensive because they're very proud of the work I do. Even so, after I left that Christmas to cover the tsunami and since I have swooped into and out of the house much the same way in the years since, the kids nicknamed me Mommy Tsunami.

Yes, as a mother—and in my job—I am constantly being stretched like Gumby among national security, breaking news, and events that I have no control over.

Recently, I had two simultaneous breakfast meetings scheduled in the Washington, DC, Four Seasons dining room. One was business, and the other, a few tables away, was personal—with a group of my friends and other women who are all journalists. Mary Louise Kelly from NPR had just published a book, *It. Goes. So. Fast: The Year of No Do-Overs*, about trying to juggle motherhood and reporting. How ironic.

In her speech to our group, she said, "We moms know that you can't be in two places at one time."

I wanted to put my hand up and say, "Actually, I am right now! I'm here for breakfast with you all, and I'm also reporting on the Kremlin on my phone under the table."

But that is our life. Of course, if we don't laugh, we'll cry, right?

I've also found during the last twenty-two years, since I first gave birth, that I will get urgent simultaneous calls that the kids need something *and* there's a major national security event.

I'll never forget when Luke was in kindergarten and it was picture day at school. He had forgotten his bow tie. He was really into bow ties, so I got a call from the teacher saying, "Luke really needs you to bring his bow tie." At that exact moment, I got an alert that the US military had dropped the MOAB, the Mother of All Bombs, in eastern Afghanistan against an ISIS training camp. So there I was, trying both to be a mother and to report on the mother of all bombs. And what was my decision? Should I go straight to the Pentagon to get closer to the live-shot position to get on air, or should I take an extra fifteen minutes to take Luke his bow tie, so he has it for picture day?

I'll do both.

I took Luke his bow tie.

And of course, I made it to work in time; I might have even broken the news. I know I got on air pretty darn fast and didn't miss a beat. I've never missed a live shot in twenty-eight years of working for FOX.

It's not that we as mothers don't feel stress while trying to do it all, but I wouldn't have it any other way. Yes, I'm always running late for things, always trying to be in two places at once, but somehow I get there at the right moment. I may be walking into the Pentagon late or the last parent to show up at a performance, but I am there.

It has happened over and over—and it is *because* I'm a mother that I have been able to do all that I do. I believe that being a mother in the Middle East was a key part of my achieving success as a journalist and building trust with the people I was reporting on. It gave me a degree of compassion, authenticity, and an ability to understand people.

I think that my being a mother was humanizing and the great equalizer.

I also think that just as my mother influenced me, I'm handing down that love of culture and a larger worldview to my kids. We have spent quality time around the dinner table for years, engaging in conversation about our days, and often graced by the presence of friends and others who have brought stories from around the world.

Annalise often tells her friends, "I can't call my mom right now. There is breaking news." My kids not only place their calls based on the news cycle but follow the news closely and are also now deeply engaged in world events. They did volunteer work in high school to support Afghanistan because of our family's vested interest in the country and are studying foreign affairs in college with an eye toward public/government service. That makes me extremely proud.

In 2022, after I had just lived through covering the chaotic and emotional withdrawal of US military forces from Afghanistan, my daughter Amelia called me at the Pentagon. "Mom, you have to do something. We have to set up a GoFundMe for the Afghans," she said, concerned about the suffering.

Like all my kids, Amelia has a big heart, and although she knew that I was busy in the Pentagon, I was there to answer her call and proud to know that the people I have spent my career reporting on have captured her compassion and she wants to help.

So to every young producer, TV correspondent, and person in any other profession who wonders, "How can I do both?" or worries if it will affect your children if you do, I always give the same advice: try.

If I have learned anything in all these years covering war *and* peace, it's this: life gets in the way of our plans. I've had some amazing experiences, and I love my career—but being a mom is the best thing that ever happened to me.

CHAPTER 12

Annette Hill

Licensed Professional Counselor

"Suit up, show up, and see what God has planned
for you today."

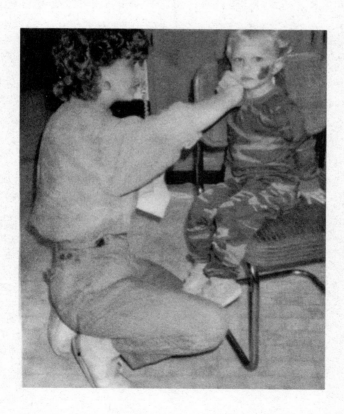

I've known Annette since I was a child. When she went back to school to become a licensed clinical therapist as an adult, my mom was her clinical supervisor and mentor. Their professional relationship soon turned into a deep friendship following a tragedy in Annette's life. I am grateful that she entered both of our lives. Not only did Annette put herself through school as a single mother, but she has been through the most unimaginable tragedy for a mom: the loss of her child. Yet when Annette reflected on whether she is still a mother now that she no longer has a child, her answer was a resounding yes. Ever since her loss, she has poured all her energy into caring for other mothers' children, notably young people and veterans.

Annette has written the mental health treatment program for veterans and first responders at Warriors Heart in San Antonio, Texas, among other places, and presents programs to law enforcement and military agencies around the country. Through it all, she has gained strength from her faith, and in my opinion, her faith has moved mountains.

Between both of our schedules, finding a time to sit down and chat was difficult. When we finally connected, it was over Memorial Day weekend. Annette put it best: "That's God. It happens over and over, and I just don't think it's an accident that we are having this conversation on the day we celebrate the lives lost from military sacrifice."

Finding Our Way

Before I became a therapist, I was an interior designer. Ironically, being a therapist is not dissimilar; I'm still doing interior design, now it's just between the ears.

At the time, I was in my early twenties and married to a Scottsdale, Arizona, police officer. Even though I was using contraceptive, I became pregnant. What's sad but truthful is that I considered not remaining pregnant; I was only twenty-one, and I wasn't sure I was ready to be a mother.

I knew I had a medical predisposition that made me prediabetic, but at that age, I didn't understand the impact the condition would have on me during pregnancy. Ultimately, I made the decision to keep my baby, and my son, Adam Gibson Hill, was born on October 4, 1984. He was five and a half weeks early and had many potential complications due to my medical condition. Technically, though he weighed eight pounds and came five and a half weeks early, only his large size (thus early birth) was due to the type 1 prediabetes. His premature birth was the cause of a high bilirubin level, which concerns brain and lung immaturity.

Even the delivery had been difficult. Adam was in the NICU, and I underwent several surgeries to fix the damage from a traumatic delivery. Thankfully, Adam and I both recovered fine, but the experience made me decide not to have another child. But I was glad I did make the decision to be a mom. For that, it was all worth it. I was so amazed at the little bundle of life I had brought into the world—and then he became my world.

From the minute Adam came out of the womb, everything about him was "go." He was always on the move. He wanted to be involved in the world, and he never hid behind my skirts. In short, he gave me a run for my gosh-dang money.

My little boy was sweet, funny, and very verbal. Right from birth, you can see the temperament of your kid, and Adam had some of those classic boy traits. By age four he chewed his toast into the shape of a gun and loved G.I. Joe and LEGOs. He also made friends easily, so our condo was where everyone wanted to be—and I loved that.

Just shy of Adam's fifth birthday, his father and I divorced. We loved each other, we just weren't in love anymore. I became Adam's primary caregiver but wasn't making much money as an interior designer, even though I was working full-time. I was struggling financially. Adam's dad made a good living so was able to take him on the "fun" vacations. All that mattered was that Adam had fun and got those experiences, because I couldn't give them to him.

As Adam and I were finding our way as a little family, growing our faith became important to me. A nearby nondenominational charismatic-type church welcomed me in and didn't ostracize me for being divorced. It was my first connection to a church. My mom was Catholic and my dad was Baptist, but when they'd had kids, they had chosen not to expose us to religion. The church asked if I'd lead a divorce recovery group seminar, then a singles group, then women's ministries. Eventually I became a nonpaid lay counselor for a bunch of people based on my own experiences. In that new role, I discovered something about myself: I liked to teach. I also realized that I liked doing research and figuring out how and why the brain does what it does. Little did I know that my desire to understand the brain and behavior would be vital to my survival in the next few years.

In 1994, when Adam was twelve, I was physically attacked and had to deal with the lingering trauma, which started with having nightmares every night. I went to the Center Against Sexual Assault (CASA) in Phoenix for counseling. I had never even heard of post-traumatic stress disorder (PTSD). After four months of therapy, I wasn't any better. I still had nightmares. My dad was an alcoholic, and this new trauma opened the door to a lot of bad feelings I had buried my whole life. But I didn't want to take medicine; I wanted the therapist to help me fix it without medications.

The therapist said, "Let's try Eye Movement Desensitization and Reprocessing [EMDR] to get into the subconscious and emotional parts of the brain."

At that point I was willing to try anything, so we started.

After the first session of EMDR, my nightmares stopped. I kept seeing the therapist and cleaned up the trauma so I could move forward in my life.

Say Yes

A few weeks later, around Thanksgiving, Adam was playing with his LEGOs, and I had a moment of clarity while sitting on the couch nearby.

I asked myself, "If I wasn't so afraid, what would I do with my life?" That question stemmed from a well-documented phenomenon called "post-traumatic growth." I had always been anxious; that was why we never took vacations. I was always afraid we wouldn't have enough money one day, so I needed to save. I was always afraid.

I decided I'd stop saying no to new things out of fear. I made a pact with myself: *Just say yes.*

As I thought about the question I had asked, the idea came to me that I would become a psychotherapist. After fifteen years in interior design, I was tired and over it. Now I needed to go back to school while also supporting our little twosome.

After creating a bottom-line budget, I quit my job, enrolled in university, and started my own little catering business making healthy to-go lunches. I called it Better Box Lunch after Ralph Waldo Emerson's advice to "build a better mousetrap."

I was nervous but exhilarated by the unknown. It was exciting because it was all mine and all up to me. I said *yes*.

Every morning I would get up at four, make the lunches—it was all gourmet food, presented beautifully on glass dishes—then drive Adam to school and deliver the lunches around town. Then I came home, did my homework, picked Adam up, and bought ingredients at the store for the next day. I fed Adam dinner, went to night school, came home, and did the whole thing again in the morning. I had no medical insurance, and I had to budget and pray a lot, but God met my needs to the penny every month.

Still, each year on the anniversary of the sexual assault, I would fall apart and I often cried or drank too much. In 1999, at the end of undergraduate school, I finally realized that I would have to work through forgiveness to be free from the trauma. I had made the decision not to give up on God after the attack and still went to church, but I had not let go of my anger toward the man who had hurt me.

So I had a conversation with God about it, and at the end of it, I said, "I'm giving my anger to You; I can't handle it anymore."

At the right moment, He presented to me His plan for how I would move forward.

My friend Lesley updated me about a little girl named Elaine, suffering from cystic fibrosis, whom I had met years before at Lesley's Christmas party. Elaine had two months to live unless she received a lung transplant from a live donor. She was only fourteen, the same age as Adam. I was in my midthirties and very athletic, so my lungs were healthy. I also had O-negative blood, which is rare and the reason why I have literally donated gallons and gallons of it in my lifetime. I offered to be tested, and it turned out that I was a match for Elaine. I donated my left lower lung lobe, and her uncle Sam, a SWAT cop in Seattle, donated part of his right. I'm now known as "lefty," and Sam is "righty." It was a hearty competition for who would perform better. We tried to focus on that, as by the surgery date Elaine had only two weeks to live.

The day I learned I was a match was the anniversary of my assault. That stuck with me because I had just had my big forgiveness conversation with God.

Elaine was at Children's Hospital Los Angeles, so we flew to California from Arizona. The day of the surgery, September 16, was the anniversary of my baptism at church ten years earlier. I knew God had heard my prayer and this was the moment to claim back my life while saving hers. The surgery left me with a nine-inch scar on my back and missing a portion of rib and the bottom half of my left lung—but it's worth it because Elaine survived and is still thriving.

My mom stayed with Adam while I was gone. After the surgery, she told me that it had scared him; he'd been afraid I'd die. I felt bad, but I knew that one day he'd understand. I'd also missed his first day of high school because of the transplant. But I knew that there would be many other celebrations to share with him during his life.

After three years, I sold the catering business to pay for graduate school. All of my hard work was paying off. Life was good.

G.I. Joe

When 9/11 happened, Adam was a sophomore in high school and, like so many other young men, was inspired to join the military to help protect his country. So six weeks after he graduated from high school in 2003, I said an emotional goodbye as he headed off. He was assigned to the 172nd Stryker Brigade in Fairbanks, Alaska. I missed him terribly.

In August 2005, he was deployed to Iraq. He wore a camera on his shoulder at all times and sent me SD cards full of photos because he knew his mom needed to know where he was and that he was all right. I was proud of him for wanting to serve his country, but as a mother it was hard wondering if he would be okay from one minute to the next.

It was probably for the best that I was busy during that time, finishing my studies and training. I was working at Devereux Advanced Behavioral Health, a counseling center for low-income kids, many of whom were in foster care. Becky Martin, Nicole's mom, was my supervisor. We became fast friends, and she has been a huge support system in my life.

A year later I was thrilled because Adam was back in Kuwait and scheduled to come home. The Strykers had been stripped of their weapons and were set to be shipped back to Alaska. But my joy bubble burst when the theater command sergeant major flew into Kuwait and told Adam's brigade that they were not going home. Adam was instead sent to Baghdad for "the push." His was the first brigade that had to extend their tour; unfortunately, there would be many thereafter.

I didn't know how much more those young men could handle. They'd already suffered a lot of deaths and many IED explosions and injuries. Once again, I worried and prayed that Adam would remain unharmed and return to me.

Two tours and seventeen months later, I was elated when Adam set foot back on US soil. But he was different; they were all different. He drank heavily, and I indulged it because I knew he had been through things I will never have to see. After he returned home, he lived with me for four months, and he stayed in his room much of the time. He played video games, and he slept a lot and had frequent nightmares.

I thought, "Let him sleep. There will be other events and holidays to celebrate. He needs to rest." At that point in my profession, I knew enough about the brain to know what happens when you don't get enough sleep. In battle, those young men had had no days off and had been awake all but four hours a day. They had catnapped in holes on the desert floor, anywhere they could—all while guys they knew were lying maimed or dying beside them.

The bubbly child I'd known was somewhere else. Adam had a hundred-yard stare that looked past me, not seeing me. The child who had always been focused on human connection didn't seem to connect with me or anyone else anymore.

One day he said to me, "I see you, Mom, but it's like I'm living through plexiglass. I can see you, but I can't touch you, I can't feel you."

He had been diagnosed with PTSD when he had first returned to the States, in the four-month decompression and transition period at Fort Riley, Kansas, before he had come home to Arizona. We tried to get him to go to the Veterans Administration hospital, but the VA wasn't even talking about PTSD at the time. We looked for a therapist, but he wanted a male counselor and they were in short supply, so I watched him flounder. I felt helpless.

He had gone into temporary sobriety at Fort Riley after being diagnosed with PTSD, but his sobriety faltered after he came back to Arizona. I brought it up and was relieved when he decided to stop drinking on his own.

I finally said, "We have to get you up and out. What about going back to school?"

He decided he wanted to become a cop and enrolled in the criminal justice program at the community college nearby. He started working in security with an electronics company while going to school and even got his own apartment up the street from me. He started to laugh again, and I could see glimpses of the son I had always known.

Adam was doing well at the job and in school, but even though he was now in his early twenties, it seemed to me that he was still stuck at eighteen, back before he had gone to war. He saw all his high school friends with jobs, girlfriends, and futures because in five years' time they'd moved on with their lives. And he hadn't. So one month into moving into his own apartment, Adam went online and got a girlfriend. He felt that that was the missing link. I met her only a couple of times, but I had a bad feeling. She liked to party, and I knew that was not good for my son.

A Recipe for Disaster

A few months later, I was en route back from San Diego from Elaine's ten-year transplant celebration party, and I called Adam to chitchat on the long drive.

His vehicle had been T-boned by a big truck, totaling Adam's car, and the next day, he said, "She left me, she left me!" He was sobbing, and it sounded as though he was drinking. I kept him on the phone the entire drive back.

When I got to his apartment, I saw an empty bottle of hard liquor. They were fighting—again. I knew Adam and his girlfriend both liked guns, and each had weapons in the apartment. It's not uncommon for veterans to own weapons, but in my line of work, I like to remove them when a situation is tense.

I said, "People fight, you'll be fine. Let me take your gun until things settle down."

I was relieved that he gave it to me. I took him home with me, made him a meal, and had him sleep in his old bedroom. I hoped he would sleep it off and have perspective in the morning and realize she wasn't good for him. I took him to get a rental car, and when we spoke later in the day, he said she had come home and things between them were fine. But immediately after that major auto accident, he was notably more overwhelmed. It was as though the pin had come out of the grenade. And the compression of significant events just prior and to follow made it very much worse.

A few days later, Adam turned twenty-five. We had dinner to celebrate, and his girlfriend was at the dinner. I saw an opportunity to try to intervene. Privately, I said to her, "You two fight, and you drink. Please take your gun out of the apartment. Also, the drinking is not good for Adam; he must go into sobriety again."

She balked at removing her weapon but agreed to my suggestion to keep it in her vehicle instead. And I knew she wasn't going to support Adam giving up alcohol mainly because she had recently told him, "I want to be with someone who can party." A few days after his birthday, she drove to Colorado to visit family and friends. She took her gun along in her bag.

Adam decided he would go to Colorado as well and accompany her on the long ride back. On October 16, I begrudgingly took him to the airport and dropped him off. He stayed with her in Colorado for a couple of days; then they drove home together.

Thursday, October 22, Adam confronted his girlfriend about suspicions that she was being unfaithful. She reassured him that he was the one she wanted to be with. On Friday, October 23, she told Adam she was going out to a party that night and left him home alone. When she got home, she saw he had been drinking the whole evening. When they woke up later the next day, they went for a drive to the DMV to put one of her two vehicles into Adam's name.

As Adam was driving, she suddenly said, "I'm going to get my own apartment."

He was stunned and asked, "Are you breaking up with me?" He instantly panicked, turned the car around, and drove home as they argued. Her bags from the trip were still packed and just inside the apartment—with her gun inside them. They continued arguing, and he went into her luggage.

Suddenly, in an instant, he was gone.

They had been dating only eight months.

Adam died at noon from a self-inflicted gunshot wound from her gun. I would not find that out until five that afternoon after they finished questioning his girlfriend, who was still in the apartment. Her affair partner showed up before Adam's body was even removed from the apartment.

I, on the other hand, hadn't seen Adam since dropping him off at the airport to go to her. A week later, after Adam's funeral, I found out all the details of that day from the detective who had found Adam lying on his apartment floor.

The entire time Adam was on the battlefield, I had convinced myself that it was highly possible that I might never see him again and that I would be informed, in person, by two army soldiers at my door. I wasn't remotely prepared for two police officers, two firefighters, and one detective standing on my front porch delivering the most horrifying sentences a person can hear. Not now, not this way.

I'd had no idea when I'd dropped Adam off, said goodbye to him, and watched him walk through the airport doors that it would be the last time I saw him.

Shockingly, I did see him again, but it was at the funeral home before he was cremated. I knew it would be the last time I would ever see his beautiful face. Burned into my memory is the fact that I was wearing red lipstick, and in my effort not to stop saying goodbye, I just kept kissing him all over his forehead and cheeks and face. My baby. My precious son.

Adam's favorite holiday was Halloween, and it was an irony that due to the timing of his death, one week later was the thirty-first. A year before, I'd been putting Joker makeup on him for a costume party. So much can change in just a year.

I would later learn that my son's death had been the result of a recipe that's common for veterans and active-duty servicemen and -women and is at the root of the oft-stated statistic that there are twenty-two suicides a day among service members. Twenty-two. Mental health professionals all believe the number to be higher, just underreported. These service members attempt to live with the underlying trauma of their jobs, and when they experience many difficult events tightly clustered together, they are pushed to the breaking point. Most of us have a tough time bearing up under such things. But when one is also dealing with significant unresolved trauma, it can result in snapping. Twenty-two suicides a day. A compression of situations in their lives floods them to the point that they are mentally overwhelmed by a sense of being trapped and alone.

Six months before his own death, two of Adam's friends died of overdose and suicide. He was prepping for midterms in college, and he was also promoted at work, which was great, but it came with more responsibility. His girlfriend told him she didn't want to be with a guy who wouldn't party with her; therefore he started drinking again. And last, he discovered that she was unfaithful to him. It's a toxic mix. When you are living with PTSD, your base activation state is higher than if you weren't harboring trauma. So when external factors begin to build up, it doesn't take as much to push you over the edge.

For more than 60 percent of veterans and first responders who commit suicide, a relationship crisis is the last straw and often the last moment of life. In any relationship, your guard is down with the one person you think you can be honest with—after all, you *chose each other*. But if a person is struggling with life pressures and other things, it makes it more difficult for a love relationship to flourish.

Adam suffered not just from PTSD but from unresolved grief/loss and moral injury, as so many in the military and the first responder community do. The symptoms overlap. In the military and law enforcement people are made to do and see things they didn't consider when they signed up and joined the ranks. All the pain of that is carried and becomes a filter of the present when it is not addressed. And they feel guilt as though they own all the responsibility, when in reality they don't. When Adam was drinking at home, I'd hear fragments of the things he'd done and seen and the pain he carried.

I should have been able to save that woman.

I should have been able to stop that IED.

It should have been me instead of my buddy.

The unresolved loss and grief can be overwhelming.

Knowing that didn't help and on some level made it worse for me. It was so unfair. I was so angry. I said to God, "So let me get this right: in Elaine's moment of crisis, I stepped up to the plate and gave her my lung. And nobody stepped in to save my son in that last moment of crisis?"

After Adam died, we had one week to clean his belongings out of his apartment. I saw the holes in the door and the carpet cut out where he had been lying. I didn't know how to handle the death of my son in that room, that way. I sat all by myself right where he had died and prayed. I said, "I want every little piece of you to come with me, all of this pain to come with me. You are not staying here, Adam. You are coming home with me."

Planning Adam's funeral was surreal. I dreaded facing the five hundred people who would be there. Even though I had some thoughts about ending my own life, I couldn't. I had to show up for my son.

At the funeral, I said, "We always know how old our kids are. Twenty-four months, three and a half years, and so on. I am going to continue with that. So my son is twenty-five years and twenty days—*and seven Jesus days today.*"

From that day, I started counting his Jesus days. I still do.

Grieving

Dealing with grief is a tricky thing. I struggled with the fact that the underlying cause of Adam's death was my area of professional specialty. By that point I was certified to care for trauma patients, and I had been unable to save my own son. Who would ever want to be treated by me? I had built a new life wanting to help others, and in an instant, my entire life and identity had been shattered.

I contemplated suicide myself. I still had Adam's weapon, after all, and hey, who would blame me?

Soon after Adam's death, someone told me I was now a Gold Star mom. I thought, "How insensitive! I don't want a gold sticker! I just want my son back."

I had to go back to work just ten days after losing my son. The bills don't stop arriving just because your world is caving in. But I found that going to work, for an hour at a time I was able to focus on my client, and it slowed down my own grief so I could get my bearings—so when the waves of horrifying emotions came back, I had my sea legs.

I slept in Adam's room and went through the motions. I worked and went home.

The first anniversary of his death, I had to face a string of numbing anniversaries in just the month of October: his birthday on the fourth, the last time I saw him on the sixteenth, his death on the twenty-fourth, and his funeral on Halloween. The other holidays and benchmarks throughout the year weren't any easier. Every time I turned around, there was something to remind me that my son would never again be there to participate in anything.

My mom was overwhelmed; she didn't know what to say to help. I don't blame her. By that point she had aged, and her life was very small. She had moved into an anxious phase and was dealing with her own pain. She was supportive and did what she could, but after Adam's death, my supervisor and friend, Becky, was the one who showed up at my door. Becky took that burden off my mom and took on the big-sister role with me. Friends and colleagues really looked out for and kept wrapping around me. They helped me through.

After three years of that, I had a firm conversation with myself. I needed to find a way to stop living in despair. So I started a gratitude journal, a technique I had learned in therapy years before. You buy a notebook that you like to look at because it must always be by your bedside. At the end of each day, you have to write down five things from that day that you're grateful for—no sweeping statements, it has to be specific things from that day. If you forget one day, you must write ten things the next.

"What fires together wires together"; if you're thinking only about awful things, they are all you're going to see.

Conversely, looking for something positive will help you start thinking about more positive things. You will notice that good things are, in fact, happening all around you each day. It's hard, but it makes your brain muscle work and retrain itself because you have to hold on to those positive thoughts all day long to write them down that night.

One hundred and thirty-five days into the process, I started to feel like myself again. It dawned on me that if I had not done that trauma work all those years before, I would not have had the tools to survive this catastrophic trauma.

I took another step and decided to join the Gold Star community; I didn't realize that it had started during World War I. A Bronze Star symbolizes meritorious service in combat, and a Silver Star reflects heroic valor. A Gold Star is bestowed when a person dies in combat or because of war, and PTSD, which is a physiological injury, if left untreated can result in a war fatality.

Every year there's a nationwide barbecue where the families congregate and honor their fallen loved ones. It's beautiful and eventually becomes healing for the grieving loved ones. October was looming, but instead of drawing the blinds and crying, I thought, "I should host the Gold Star barbecue in my backyard, because if it's here in this backyard, I will have to hold it together."

That was another step in the process of getting my life onto a type of solid ground. Instead of living in the netherworld of despair and grief, I had to focus on the earthly present. It began with landscaping my yard to prepare for the barbecue, and I have been hosting ever since.

Someone had given me a Bible in high school, and at age seventeen I decided to flip it open to a random page. It was the Book of Job. Soon after Adam died, I sat outside and purposefully opened it to Job. I needed to read about someone else who had felt so unmoored and cried out to God. It was as if God was letting me know I wasn't alone, and when it was really bad, He was still there. About ten years earlier, when getting involved in the church, I had decided to read the Bible cover to cover. I read one book from the Old Testament and then one from the New Testament. I started noticing that the questions in one book were eventually answered in the other. I came away realizing that the Bible is about a bunch of misfits; it's only God's intervention that is good and with purpose.

I started the mountainous grieving process by looking at photos of Adam's face and listening to his voice on video by viewing all of those SD cards he had sent home from Iraq. I know moms who won't look at their kids' photos; they turn pictures down. But I knew that if a person doesn't stay connected to how their loved one lived, they will remain stuck in the darkness of how they died.

The realization came that I had all that history from Adam's time in Iraq—of my son *and* all those other young men. I took my computer to the store and told the young guys working there that my son was an Iraq veteran who had passed away and I needed help turning the content into a DVD. They had friends in Iraq, too, and their eyes teared up as they said of course they would help.

To hear Adam's laugh, to see that, helped me stop thinking about his very worst day, and I started remembering and holding on to all the good days.

Releasing

There are all kinds of things I've done to symbolically both release and hold on to Adam. He started a journal in Iraq. I take it to the national cemetery in Arizona where he's laid to rest, and I write to him. An open letter.

Adam gave me a diamond necklace he'd bought in Iraq, "for all the Mother's Days and holidays I've missed." I put it on then and have never taken it off. Mother's Day is hard; you're still a mom. You'll always be a mom. But I questioned that at first.

After my second Mother's Day and a very bad night, I was pacing around my table, sobbing, talking to God. I said, "I can't make it through another Mother's Day, God. You're going to have to do something."

At two o'clock in the afternoon my phone rang, and it was someone I had met through Gold Star connections, an Iraq war veteran. He said, "I wanted to tell you about Operation Freedom Bird because I think you would be perfect for it. Would you want to come to our board meeting?"

I reminded myself that years before, I had promised myself to stop saying "no" to new things.

Just say yes. Applying that rule again, I became the clinical lead at Operation Freedom Bird, an organization aimed at reducing the symptoms of PTSD, unresolved grief, and loss. Each year, OFB takes fifty Arizona combat vets from all branches and all wars to Washington, DC, for a four-day "healing journey." That first year, during the day, we went to war memorials, and at night, we sat with the veterans, discussing trauma and moral injury. They said things they'd never said out loud to anyone. For me to be able to hear them helped in understanding what had been going on in Adam's head. No wonder he's gone. I am not sure I could live with all of that in my head and heart, either.

On Veterans Day we walked into the Pentagon, following the same path along which the plane went in on 9/11. On my back, I wore the rucksack Adam had worn in Iraq, full of symbolic things of his. I walked into the center of the Pentagon, along with the rest of the vets, and we left all the symbolic items brought in the rucksacks there. When we walked out, I felt some of the burden lifted.

Operation Freedom Bird was healing for me and others in so many ways. I made that trip for many years. At the end of each trip, I'd produce a DVD of the journey, reminiscent of the one with Adam's pictures and videos, to be given to each of the guys.

I have continued working with veterans and first responders since then, in various settings from private practice one-on-one counseling to residential treatment centers.

Signs

Back when Adam was nine, he started to understand the abstract concept of death and realized that his dad had a dangerous job as a police officer. So one day he came home after spending the weekend at his dad's and wanted to talk.

He said, "My dad could die on duty, and actually, so could you. So whenever we leave each other, I don't want to say 'I love you' anymore, because if one of us dies, the last thing we'll be saying is *you*. I just want to say 'love.' Because then if one of us dies, then the last thing we say is *love*."

I looked at my brilliant, intuitive little boy and wondered where that wisdom had come from—and from that day forward, there was one word we always said last.

Love.

Goodnight.

Love.

See you later.

Love.

He signed his cards and all his letters from Iraq that way.

Love.

That last week of Adam's life, we were bickering on text because he was stressed and I was frustrated with trying to help get him a replacement vehicle for the one that had been totaled, with his relationship situation, and with the fact that he was drinking to cope. So we didn't say "love" at the end of our messages.

Later I couldn't bear that we hadn't.

Ten days after his funeral, my close friend Lesley said, "We have to get you out of the house." She took me to lunch, and we cried for hours. I had Adam's necklace on, as I always do.

I was so angry with myself, thinking about not having said "love" to Adam in his final days. My emotions were overwhelming. I didn't know how I would move on. When I got to the parking lot after saying goodbye to my friend, there was a swath of empty spaces, yet a lone car was parked right next to mine. I stopped short and could hardly catch my breath when I saw it. On the back windshield was a decal with one word on it.

Love.

Above the word "love" it looked like a lipstick kiss, just like my red goodbye kisses on Adam's face the last time I had seen him.

I burst into tears again. Suddenly a young woman, about the age of Adam, got out of the car, and all I could see was the necklace she had on, a long chain with two crosses hanging from it.

I thought, "I'm not crazy. That's God and Adam talking to me and telling me to keep an eye out for the signs."

Since that day, I have had many more signs. I know God and Adam are both with me.

Later, a retired Delta Force Operator, who is also a part of Mission 22, named after the veteran daily suicide statistic, reached out to me. Mission 22 was building a War at Home Memorial. It would be made up of twenty five-by-ten-foot steel cutout silhouettes, each of a veteran, from all wars, male and female, who had taken their own life. Tom asked if Adam could be included in the memorial. I didn't want Adam to be the poster child for suicide. I initially said no. But God had a way of reminding me of my pact for healing all those years ago.

Say yes.

So I did.

When the silhouettes were finally up, I went to visit. I walked out and was overwhelmed to see a towering silhouette of my Adam. He's standing on his Stryker, holding out his hand in a familiar posture. They had taken a photo I had given them to cut the silhouette, and it was eerie how much it looked as though he was motioning to me.

The first time I viewed the silhouette, it was lying down on the tarmac at a runway on the property of Warriors Heart where small planes could land. I sobbed, frankly making animal noises. I started to say to the man who was tasked with taking me out there private things about the last time I had seen Adam before his cremation. The man, a thirty-year, highly decorated veteran, spontaneously began to share personal details about his worst day in combat. That man, Greg, in the four months since we had met, spoke more words than "Yes, ma'am, no, ma'am" for the first time. We bonded over the pain, and over the next weeks and months, we walked and talked, became friends, and then fell in love.

Out of that moment, it was as if my son's hand—and God's—handed me over to Greg. In the midst of pain, it's hard for us to see that all these little, beautiful moments and signs in our lives are not just coincidences. They are threaded together in a pattern and when you look back on it, you realize God was always there.

On April 3, 2021, Greg and I married. We rushed the wedding date for my mother, who was ill, but sadly, she was not well enough to travel across town to be there. Eight days after we exchanged vows, she passed away. Now Mother's Day carries a double loss, but I refuse to stay in that darkness.

I don't care for the commonly stated sentiment "Everything happens for a reason." Try telling a foster child that there's a reason someone harmed or left them. However, if one permits it, *meaning, change, and purpose* can be found if you let God take you and lead you to healing. You have to look at your narrative to heal. Sometimes we don't have words about what we feel to put into a cohesive, realistic narrative. I had to dig deep and explore all the factors involved before I could heal. I do get a piece of the blame for Adam's death; I (along with his father) blew up Adam's family when he was not even five. Iraq, the bad guys, the girlfriend all get a piece. And Adam gets a piece because he knew he shouldn't have been drinking.

Once you accept the narrative, no matter how painful, you have to set it down. You can set it down in a rucksack or a journal. But *learning* from it is key. You can't just walk away as though it never happened. It did happen, and adapting to that reality is necessary for healing. There isn't much to be gained by staying stuck in pain. And staring at it as your only view isn't going to change the fact that it happened.

So suit up, show up, and see what God has planned for you today.

I try to show up for Adam every day. I continue to work with veterans and first responders, in the hope that I can help another mother's child. I want to spread the fact that PTSD is not a permanent condition and that with focused work, the brain will learn, adapt, and heal. In my private practice, I work with teens and young adults who are struggling and whose parents don't know how to communicate with them. If they can't put into words how they are feeling, that's not good. So focus your mom—or dad—energy and let your children know you're there for them, no matter what they are going through. Just listen, and encourage your kids to talk to you.

Talk about everything.

Take too many pictures.

Keep all the letters.

Be grateful for every single moment.

And no matter what, say *love*.

CHAPTER 13

Alicia Hall

Mother of Three; FOX News Correspondent
Benjamin Hall's Wife

"We are all one another's teachers."

Late February 2022 was the last time I interviewed Benjamin Hall on television before he was nearly killed by Russian bombs during his coverage of the war in Ukraine. Though I had revered his war coverage for the seven-plus years I had worked with him, it wasn't until after that fateful day that another Hall became a hero in my eyes: his wife, Alicia.

Alicia was born in Sydney, Australia, and grew up in London, where her career kept her busy until she was reintroduced to a childhood friend, Benjamin Hall, whom she married in July 2015. Embracing the role of full-time mom to their three small children, Alicia was thrust into the position of navigating their lives after her husband's vehicle had been hit by Russian military drones while he was reporting from Ukraine on March 14, 2022, at the start of the Russian invasion. During his evacuation and the touch-and-go hours afterward, Alicia's extraordinary strength kept their family going in London while Benjamin remained in a different country for six months, undergoing extensive surgeries and recovering from the traumatic, lifelong injuries he sustained.

Alicia is a wise soul and an exceptional mother. Her strength and positive outlook are truly inspiring. Her moral compass has kept her grounded throughout her life.

Meeting Benji

In my late twenties, I moved back to London to expand my family's business outside Australia, running production and sales. One night in 2011, I was on my way to a birthday dinner for my very good friend when I bumped into an acquaintance I barely knew who was hanging with a friend outside the art gallery close by. As I was walking past, we exchanged pleasantries and he politely introduced me to the person standing next to him, Benjamin Hall.

Benji and I went to the same primary school from six to eight years old in London, but such is the nature of life that we had lost touch as we grew up. The fact that we ran into each other again after all those years had passed reminds you that sometimes things are just meant to be; our stories are already written.

A few days after we met, he reached out to me, and we went on a couple of dates. I wasn't in the headspace to date seriously, as I was focused on everything I was trying to accomplish with the family business. I traveled a lot, and he did, too, as he was doing mostly freelance writing at the time in conflict zones around the world. Still, he was persistent, and I enjoyed being around him, so we maintained a close friendship throughout the next year. Eventually we began going out.

After that, our relationship moved quite quickly. We soon began talking about having a family. I wanted children and so did Benji, and we both believed that despite his at times rather risky career, it would be the next part of our journey together. Because family is everything.

A Strong Family

My grandfather was Austrian Jewish, and at the beginning of World War II, his family escaped from Austria to Australia, where he met my New Zealand–born grandmother. My father was born and raised in Sydney. My British mother was born and raised in

Mumbai, India, by English parents, growing up in Colonial India in the 1950s. She eventually met my father in London whilst she was at drama school. Together they moved to Sydney, where they began their shoe-manufacturing business, later moving myself and my two sisters with them back to London when I was six years old. Some people ask if moving to another country during childhood is hard, but I think moving is healthy for children and adults alike. It challenges you and forces you to create a new world for yourself—to meet new people, learn new cultures, and adapt to new situations as seamlessly as possible. Change is good. It makes you stand on your own two feet and teaches you the importance of your family and friendships and how important it is to build that network of support around you. My family's and friends' support was invaluable to me when Benji's accident happened, and I have never felt more proud of, and grateful for, every single person in my world. During a time of fear and darkness, I experienced so much love and support from the most wonderful people.

Growing up, I had very present parents. They were self-employed, so they had the luxury of being able to prioritize our upbringing, and between the two of them they were always there for us. That was a lesson I learned from them early on: family is important, and every day is a day not to be missed no matter how insignificant. If you are fortunate enough to be able to be with your children, be there. Enjoy it. And learn from them, too—they will be your greatest teachers.

I decided to go back to Australia for university and studied visual communications, which led me to working on the production side of television in Australia before joining the family business and moving back to London. That was when Benji and I crossed paths again.

When you finally realize that you want to build a family—and whom you want to build it with—it can happen fast. We loved each other and it felt right, and when Benji proposed to me, of course I said yes.

And so we got married in London on July 3, 2015, in the Brompton Oratory Catholic church in Knightsbridge. It was a lovely, happy day as we exchanged vows, promising to always be there for each other in sickness and in health.

Priorities Change

Soon we had our first child, Honor, and that day was the first day of our new life. Nothing could have prepared me for that feeling that nothing was more important than she was; her well-being and happiness were of utmost importance, and the day she was born was the day I knew my family would become my full-time job.

The day after Honor was born was Benji's first full day with the FOX News bureau in London, and he quickly began traveling the world, covering conflicts, natural disasters, terrorist attacks, and more, which meant that he often had to drop everything and leave. It felt natural to be with Honor and care for her, not a chore. Up until that point, I had been so career driven, but now that I was a mum, it was the first time I ever thought, "I'd rather do this mum job."

Without realizing it, I mimic my mum. The greatest thing I learned from her is that she genuinely enjoyed bringing us up and being a mum.

I'd always known that I wanted three kids. In 2017, Iris was born, and in 2019, my dream of three children came true with the birth of our third daughter, Hero. Our family was complete.

In 2021, Benji was offered the role of State Department correspondent at FOX, based in Washington, DC. He went ahead to settle into his new role, and the plan was for the children and me to join him at the beginning of their new school year. Benji would commute between DC and London. Nothing could have prepared us for how incredibly hard that would be; Benji was a very present father, and not having him around every day put a real strain on the family unit. At the time, he was traveling a lot covering the secretary of state, Antony Blinken, and it was becoming quite clear that that would continue for the foreseeable future. I didn't love the thought of being in DC alone with the girls. When I had been young and moved from Australia to the United Kingdom, I had been with my entire family. With Benji gone, I would not only lose my London support network but have to establish a new one in a new country during a pandemic on my own. I thought that would be tricky. It was still the plan, though. However, the DC-area schools were still requiring face masks to be worn by children, and that was the deciding factor for us. I didn't want to move until the mask mandate for children in schools was lifted—I didn't want the girls to have to wear a mask in school when they didn't have to in the United Kingdom. So we delayed the girls' and my moving to the United States.

At the end of January 2022, Benji flew back to London for the girls' Christmas *Nutcracker* ballet recital, which had been delayed due to covid lockdown. That was the last weekend we were together before Benji's accident. As he was leaving the next morning, I had the strongest feeling that he wouldn't be coming home again.

A month later, while the girls and I were still in London, Russia invaded Ukraine and Benji left DC to cover the conflict.

As during every trip, we talked every day, and as during every war he covered, he was seeing terrible things that were difficult to talk about. In London, we had a lot of Ukrainian refugees arrive, and our schools accepted the children of the families who were fleeing. So we really felt quite emotionally drawn into the war, much more than with any other conflict he'd covered. All war is the same; it just felt very much more on our doorstep this time. It was hard work. And it was emotionally draining to see atrocities happening day in and day out. So many families were being torn apart. That was the hardest part, seeing fathers sending off their wives and children and staying behind to fight. It was very reminiscent of World War II, and we all struggled with it. It was a very emotional time, but as always, I felt proud that Benji was there.

He called constantly while he was away, mainly at the end of the day, when he had work breaks and the children were in bed. I would tell him about the day, and he would update me on everything he had seen. On March 13, the DC mask mandates were lifted, so that night we decided it was time for us to make the move to DC, even though he was still reporting from Ukraine. That night, I felt that change was coming.

Catastrophe

The next day, the fourteenth, I remember feeling very calm as I went about the day, but I still had a sense that everything was on the verge of changing. Even though I hadn't heard from Benji all day, it didn't seem unusual because the nature of his work is sporadic and sometimes I wouldn't hear from him until late. However, at about 5:00 p.m. UK time I still hadn't heard from him, and all the messages I'd sent to him that day had been delivered—but never read.

I began feeling as though something was definitely not right.

About that time, I got a call from Suzanne Scott, FOX News CEO. "There's been an accident, and he's critical," she said.

All I could say was, "How critical?"

She replied, "Very critical."

There wasn't much else to say, and I didn't ask questions. I felt as though Suzanne had told me everything she knew at that moment, and she promised to keep me posted as things developed. When something catastrophic occurs, everything immediately thereafter happens so quickly; you're trying to absorb it all, and you just keep moving. I immediately rang Rick, Benji's colleague who works in the same kind of industry; he already knew that something had happened to Benji because someone in his logistics group had sent him an image of Benji's press card covered in debris. It was chilling.

The shock of the news was extraordinary; of all the things you prepare for in life, I had been unprepared for this. It was the first time I felt completely powerless, knowing that the outcome would be completely out of my control. However, once the initial shock of a scenario begins to wear off, I think you do go into fight-or-flight mode—or both simultaneously.

Like most unexpected events, the phone call from Suzanne came at the busiest time of my day. Between 4:30 and 5:00 p.m. is dinner, and 7:00 p.m. is bed. I still had a two-hour window when the kids would be very much around. I'd have to go downstairs and finish my job of being their mom for the rest of the day. Luckily, my wonderful housekeeper, Lor, was downstairs. She typically does not feed or bathe them, but that night, she was able to stay and help me while I got my bearings straight. She knew that something was wrong and stepped right in.

I was reminded very quickly how wonderful humans can be; everyone helped, from my closest friends and family to people I had never even met. That was what stood out to me throughout: people are fundamentally good, and they thrive from helping others. When presented with the opportunity to do the right thing, in my experience, they all did.

From the moment I got that call, I think I went into autopilot. I knew I needed to start asking questions and alerting the family, but I didn't have much information. Benji's mom had passed away right after our middle daughter was born and his father had passed away six months before the war started, so my next call was to my sister, who immediately got onto a plane to come help me. The girls were two, four, and six years old—young enough that I was able to hide what was going on from them because I didn't want to tell them anything until I knew more about what we were facing or if he would even live.

I wasn't sure if keeping it from them was a good idea, but I did. A friend of mine who had mentioned her own experience with a family tragedy and always felt she hadn't been told soon enough urged me to tell the girls. But I decided not to because of how I felt as a mum. When she told me her story, I identified more with her mother in that instance and why her mum had delayed sharing bad news. As a mum, sometimes you just know what's right for your child, whether it makes sense to others or not. There's no rationale; you just have to listen to your instincts. You get a bit of a sixth sense with the people you love, just as I had somehow known that Benji wouldn't be coming back after the ballet recital.

So I kept moving forward, trusting that the people organizing FOX's miraculous evacuation of Benji were doing the best they could do to get him out. And they did.

A few days after the accident and once they were able to get Benji across the Polish border, Suzanne sent me a video of the helicopter carrying Benji to Landstuhl Hospital, a US Army post near Ramstein Air Base in Germany. I would then learn that Benji's vehicle had been hit by armed drones in Horenka, on the outskirts of Kyiv. That was also when I found out that Benji's two colleagues Pierre and Sasha had been killed. Benji had lain by the road for nearly an hour following the explosion, bleeding and barely conscious. Had it not been for a Ukrainian command making a wrong turn and seeing him, our life would have been very different. Again, some things are truly meant to be; a chance meeting had brought us together years before, and now another would bring him back to me.

I was beyond grateful that he had been rescued, and now that he was safe, I needed to see him. My other sister, Skye, was on holiday at the time skiing with her partner, Chris. They flew in to take care of the girls. I kept the girls home from school that day to spend time with Skye and Chris.

I said, "Girls! You're not going to school today; Skye and Chris are going to look after you all day while I do a bit of work." They were excited to see Skye. My children are so used to my looking after them that whenever anyone does they are thrilled, so they didn't even ask where I was going. I flew out of London to Germany at 6:00 a.m. and came back at eleven that night without disrupting the girls' routine at all.

I don't even remember how I got to the hospital. My mind was a blur. I knew that Benji was barely stable and had burns and other injuries from the rocket explosion, but I wasn't quite sure what I was going to see when I got there. Once I arrived, there were so many doctors and machines and a sense of urgency permeating everything. Strangely enough, Benji still looked like himself to me, because he was conscious and the essence of his spirit came through. But he had lost half his skull, the bottom half of one leg, and the foot from the other, his face was burned, and one eye was clearly terribly injured. There was so much information being given to me in such a short space of time, and all these doctors were asking me to make big decisions on his medical treatments and life. That was probably the hardest part because I knew if I was the one lying in the hospital bed, my parents would have been very involved in the decision making. I would want my parents involved because the people you trust the most are always your family, especially your mum and dad. But it was just me, and all of those medical decisions were suddenly on my shoulders. I knew absolutely nothing about his injuries, so it was a whole new learning curve.

What I did know was that the children shouldn't be privy to seeing any of it until we knew which way it was going to go. He was somewhat stable, but it was minute to minute, touch and go, and when he spoke, he didn't make much sense. But a small blessing was that he was conscious the entire time I was there, so I felt I could discuss all the decisions I was making for him with him, whether or not he absorbed much of what I was saying. It gave me comfort to be able to speak to him about it.

The biggest decision we had to make was where to send him for his recovery instead of bringing him home to the United Kingdom, where our family would be around him. Doctors always attest that patients recover best when their family is around them. I believe that; healing is a whole package, it's not just fixing an arm or growing back skin. The mind and the body have to heal together. However, my instincts told me that we had to protect the children. Benji was so injured that he would be in the ICU for most of his treatment, and the ICU is no place for children. What I had seen when I had gone to Germany to see Benji after he was evacuated to Landstuhl Regional Medical Center was not something my children should see, of that I was certain.

The best advice I was given during those first few weeks was to do my research and educate myself on the severity of Benji's injuries. I will forever be grateful to the US and UK military doctors and their expertise; they talked me through every medical step with such patience and clarity. Understanding the process Benji and I were about to embark on was essential, and I could not have found my strength without their assistance. My advice to anyone in our situation or similar would be to do the same: educate yourself, and do your re-search. Knowledge is power, and once you have the foundation of understanding, you can grab back that sense of control, which for me was invaluable.

Healing

We finally decided after many conversations that the best place to send Benji would be the Brooke Army Medical Center in San Anto-nio, Texas. Benji was incredibly lucky to be accepted there by secre-tarial designation of Secretary of Defense Lloyd Austin. The center had been set up to treat the wounded from Afghanistan and Iraq, so many of whom had been injured in the same way as Benji—by ex-plosives. The staff are the world's best in the treatment of polytrauma injuries like those Benji had sustained, and the care he received while there was exceptional.

It took ten days before Benji was finally stable enough to be cleared to make the long flight to San Antonio. Before he arrived in Texas, I spoke to his doctors there and they gave me a step-by-step program of what they were planning to do and how they were going to get him walking again.

I remember asking, "Will he be walking in six months?"

And the doctor said, "Walking? He'll be running in six months." He was so unbelievably positive about something that was not a positive scenario that he inspired me to be positive, too. The doctors took so much time to explain everything to me so I would under-stand what was happening. That in turn made me feel confident to start sharing information with the kids. So once Benji arrived in Texas and he was under the care of the US military doctors, I decided to tell the children that he had been injured. I had purposefully kept the initial stages from them so that when I told them, they would not detect any fear or sadness in my voice. I was determined that they would not let this define them. As with everything else throughout the scenario, I asked questions and listened to everyone's advice on how to approach it, gleaning different aspects that fit with my instincts about my children and applying them to my own situation.

I had been told the theory of "pebbling," that children cannot take too much information in at once, so the best way to introduce them to things is slowly. I used that approach during the first six months, from describing Benji's injuries and recovery to gently letting them know that he had lost his leg. I slowly gave them more and more details of what had happened to their father as they asked. I would point things out that we saw in the streets and in books—a lady in a wheelchair, a man on crutches, a person who had lost a limb—and slowly opened up a conversation so that the seeds were planted in their minds of what to expect.

I waited until Benji was as stable as possible in Texas before finally breaking the news, and I did so with the same theme in mind, gently and with not too much detail. The girls were all in the car, having just finished school. I said, "Just so you know, Daddy had a bit of an accident, but he's absolutely fine and there's nothing to worry about. He's going to be fine."

Honor looked worried and asked, "Is he okay?"

I said, "Do I look worried?"

She answered, "No."

I asked, "If I'm not worried, do you need to be worried?"

And she said, "No." And that was that.

Benji's recovery process in Texas was intense. His goal was to get home. My goal was to keep the girls stable throughout it all. We decided not to take the girls to Texas; there would be no benefit in doing so. Benji needed to get better, and his recovery was a full-time job.

I kept following my instincts about protecting the girls from the trauma, and until all of Benji's obvious injuries healed, I didn't let the kids see him. But we talked to him every day. We started with FaceTime every morning and night, with only audio. His face was still so damaged that I didn't want the image imprinted into their fragile little memories. As long as they could talk to him, they didn't ask to see him. As soon as his face healed, we started FaceTime with video, and they could see his face. I still hadn't told them that he had lost part of his legs or the injuries to his hand. We were slowly introducing the girls to this new daddy.

After the first hurdle of seeing him was completed, I knew I needed to start preparing them for when he would arrive home.

Out of nowhere, another English mother, married to a photojournalist who had lost both his lower legs when his tank had been struck, reached out to me. She said, "I don't do this, I'm very private, but when I saw you, I knew we needed to talk." I went to her house, and she just let me ask her questions. She had a six-year-old, too.

I approached telling the girls about the loss of Benji's leg the same way I had approached telling them about his accident, slowly pointing out the world around us and opening up a bit of conversation.

One day I just casually said, "Just so you know, Daddy lost his leg, he's got a new one. It' s much better and faster. It's called a robot leg."

They were nonplussed about that information. They asked, "Where did the old leg go?"

I said matter-of-factly, "Oh, I'm not quite sure, I don't actually know."

They accepted that and answered, "Okay. So he's got a robot leg now. Okay." And that was the end of it. They weren't upset. They were intrigued by it and accepted it. As an adult, you think that all these things are going to be such huge deals for a child, but kids are resilient as long as you communicate with them and show them you are all right.

It really does take a village to raise children, whether you are in a crisis or not. And if you are faced with one, you need all those people around you, strangers and friends. They surely got me through. Whenever anyone asked what they could do to help, my answer was always "Just do stuff for the kids." In my situation, if they were happy, I was happy; their happiness was of the utmost importance to both me and Benji.

Coming Home

Benji did the majority of his recovery at Brooke Army Medical Center, and as soon as he could be released, he would come home to finish his recovery in London. He was focused and worked so hard; all he wanted was to get home to us. And by the end of August 2022, six months after he had been injured in Ukraine, he was coming home.

We had worked so hard to keep everything together to get to that day. For the first time seeing the children, Benji wore trousers, not wanting to draw attention to his new robot leg. The girls are all so different, and their individual responses to Benji's arrival were different.

The littlest one, Hero, had no real concept of time. Her response was pure joy, and I had known that would be the case. She didn't realize how long he had been away and was only happy that he was home. Honor, our oldest, was overwhelmed with joy and tears.

Iris, our middle child, reacted in a different way, one I hadn't been expecting. I don't think she knew how to show her emotions, so she stayed mostly quiet. I wasn't worried that there would be any lasting issues, but I did feel for her because in the moment it seemed that she didn't know what to do with what she was feeling. That was hard for me as her mum because in those instances, you can't do anything, you just have to let them feel it.

But they had one important thing in common: none of the girls seemed to worry about Daddy's robot leg. All they knew was that Daddy was home.

That was all that really mattered.

Life Is Good

In January 2023, Benji returned to FOX in his first on-air appearance, picking up where he had left off.

Recently, we were looking through photos of Benji, myself, and the girls from several years ago. I don't recognize the people looking back at us in the pictures. You don't realize how much something can change you, not necessarily in a negative way, but I don't believe we are the same people we were.

Humans cope, we just do.

I'm no expert, but I do think everyone has it within them to face a challenge and get to the other side of it. I don't think everyone is given that challenge or able to recognize it to see the depth of their own strength. When situations like that arise—and in so many different forms—I genuinely believe that people will be very surprised at how much they can deal with and survive. I was. It is within all of us to cope. When tragedy strikes, it's amazing how many people will come out of the woodwork to help if you will let them. It brings out all the people who have also experienced something that has made them stronger or broken them at some point, whether you've known them or never met them before. I'm grateful for all those people, and I have learned that we are all one another's teachers.

Life can be incredibly hard and unfair. We cannot control what happens to us, but we can control how we react to it. I do believe that life is out of our control but our responses are ours to navigate. Right now, life is good; we were lucky Benji came home when so many others did not, and we are grateful for that. Our life is completely different and not how I imagined it would look, but it's still our family and that's what matters. All we can do is keep moving forward, doing the same things but in a slightly different way. In an incredibly unlucky situation, we can still find the light, and I urge everyone else to try as well. There will always be someone worse off than yourself; all we can do is make the most of our stories, as we never know what the next chapter will bring.

PART V

Acceptance

There is no such thing as "doing it all," no matter how hard we try. It is far too easy to get caught up in the fast pace of life and the demands it places on us. Before we know it, we can become depleted both mentally and physically. We can become so distracted by doing everything for everybody that we end up in no shape to care for anybody. It is important to be there for our families and our jobs; we can be there for both, but we also have to listen to our own self and accept that we cannot be everything to everyone every time.

CHAPTER 14

Martha MacCallum

Anchor and Executive Editor, *The Story with Martha MacCallum*

"Don't hesitate. Don't put life off."

From coanchoring FOX News presidential election coverage to holding debates and town halls with presidents and candidates to anchoring world events such as the funeral of Queen Elizabeth II, Martha MacCallum has been front and center on every major story on FOX News since 2004.

She began her career as a correspondent and anchor for Wall Street Journal Television. At NBC, she twice received the American Women in Radio and Television award, and she is the *New York Times* best-selling author of *Unknown Valor: A Story of Family, Courage, and Sacrifice from Pearl Harbor to Iwo Jima.* These are just a few highlights of her storied career.

One of my favorite anecdotes about Martha is from the covid pandemic in the days when we were all stuck in our remote home television studios. Given that our homes are just around the corner from each other, we shared a home studio crew. The teams went back and forth almost daily, and I felt honored to be sharing a team with the incredible Martha MacCallum. That prompted a friendship, and I am glad to have gotten to know her better off camera over recent years.

Martha is tasked with major professional responsibilities that make for long hours and travel—and through it all she has raised three children. During our interview she shared thought-provoking insights about her motherhood journey and the lessons she has learned along the way.

Just Keep Your Foot in the Door

When my kids were little, whenever someone told me my kids were polite or doing well, I always thought, "If you say that to me when they're twenty-five, then we'll really know if we got it right." Well, they're in their twenties now, and I'm watching them build their own lives, looking forward to what's ahead. I'm proud of them—and I learned many lessons along the way raising them.

Whether a mom stays at home or works, one of the biggest challenges she faces is juggling many priorities simultaneously. Obviously, as a working mom, I, too, balance a lot, and sometimes, gratefully, I have a couple of things taken off my plate while at work with a little help from others.

My mother was a big influence on me when it came to building a career. In the 1950s and '60s, she was editor of her college newspaper at Brown University; after graduating, she became a teacher for a few years, then raised three daughters. I'm the youngest. She stopped working for a while when we were young, but when I was twelve, she returned to teaching and also got her real estate license.

She really encouraged me at every step. After I had each of my three children, she reminded me that my career was part of my life and going back to work would be okay. She assured me that it would all work out. I think she saw, maybe more than I did then, that there would be some big things ahead if I hung in there. It's such a hard decision when you have a new baby looking up at you; there are many conflicting emotions. There's an overwhelming and important attachment and responsibility, so it's hard to fathom being separated from them.

I remember Mom saying to me, "Just keep your foot in the door; you might be glad you did down the road. It's much harder to pry that door open later than it is to keep it open now."

I think that most of us want the approval of our mothers. Having my mom give me the permission to do both and her reinforcement was huge for me. She was so wise, because keeping that door open enabled me to go on to so many other opportunities. Mom passed away ten years ago, and it makes me sad that she wasn't here to see the last decade of my career, because I know how much it would have meant to her.

But I'm forever grateful that she encouraged me just when I needed it the most.

Don't Look Back and Say, "I Wish I Had . . ."

When circumstances are difficult, I turn to another piece of advice my mom gave me: she always said, "Don't hesitate. Don't put life off for another time when it's more convenient to have kids or after you get this degree or after your husband gets this job."

She was right. Life is not delivered in perfect packages. It doesn't play out in tidy little chapters, and sometimes things come about that you weren't necessarily planning. When they do, I believe you must let life take its course and work your way through whatever comes to get to the other side of it. I know that that can feel like too much at times, but the alternative is missing out on so many wonderful things. My advice, particularly for young women, is, don't have to look back and say, "I wish I had . . ."

I wish I had finished that degree.
I wish I had moved or started that job.
I wish I had had children.

If you have a goal you want to achieve, this is key: ask for help when you need it. It takes a lot of support from family and friends to fulfill our dreams, particularly having children and a career at the same time. I've been really blessed, whether by my husband, my good friends, or my parents. Together, they have been my support system. I hope I have always done the same for them.

Mom is no longer with us, but her words of encouragement are still with me.

Teamwork and Responsibility

Balancing it all can become overwhelming, so it's crucial to take it one month, one week, or even one day at a time. I always try to focus on what's right in front of me and try to do it as well as I can.

However, there are inevitably days when you think, "I wish I could be in two places at once." But you can't. So you do the very best you can, and that's okay.

My husband and I both have busy lives and careers, but we have been a good tag team. When work pressures made it hard for him, I tried to step it up; he did the same for me. I believe our kids always felt that one or the other of us was accessible when they needed us. Between us, we made it to the big game, the class picnic, or the lacrosse tournament 99 percent of the time.

Many times, I'd say, "I'll step in and make sure he gets to that appointment" or "I'll take her to that dance recital because you'll be traveling." And so did he. It wasn't always easy, but our teamwork made it possible.

I taught my children that family comes first but we all have responsibilities in life, and I also think it's good for kids to understand the concept that fulfilling commitments is important. I am certain that my children benefited from my saying, "I'll be out of town next week, and you're going to have to make sure your homework is done. You're going to have to make sure you get a ride home from soccer practice on Tuesday."

I believe that in some ways it made them more capable on their own, instilling in them a sense of independence and responsibility. I always hoped that when they grew up, they'd fully appreciate those lessons, and I'm grateful that they do.

Take Care of You

I'm far from a perfect mom, and there have been times when I definitely dropped the ball.

When my youngest son finished grade school, I planned to take the day off so I could attend his graduation ceremony. I let work know it was a special day and cleared the calendar. He was so excited, and of course I wanted to be there to see it all. He had been looking forward to it for weeks.

The big day finally came. I dressed him in a little blue seersucker suit and tie, and we started out the door. Suddenly an unbelievable pain shot through the center of my body and caused me to double over. I said to my husband, "I think I need to go to the hospital. I don't know what's going on." I had never felt anything like that in my life, and I knew that something was wrong.

It was devastating to see my little boy, looking so precious, staring up at me with his face scrunched up, scared, asking me why I had to go to the hospital and not with him to his ceremony.

I was in pain, but I was also sad that the day wasn't going to be what we'd planned. Instead, a friend stepped in to take him to school, while my husband took me to the emergency room.

When we got to the hospital, I collapsed into a wheelchair. I ended up in the hospital with pancreatitis, which the doctor told me could be very serious. I was there for four days.

When gallstones had shown up on a test months before, my doctor had said to me, "You should probably take care of those before they cause a more serious problem." But it had never been convenient to carve out time to follow the doctor's recommendations and I felt fine, so I figured I'd be okay and went back to business. I soon forgot about it.

A few weeks before my son's graduation, I was out for a run, but even then, when I experienced a pain in my stomach, I just pushed through, not making the connection.

I should have paid attention to my body. I should have listened to my doctor. I felt dumb for ignoring his warning and guilty for ruining my son's special day. I learned the hard way that if we don't pay attention to our health and take the time to take care of ourselves, we are not going to be there for the people who need us at home or at work.

So, moms, don't do what I did! Take care of yourself.

My little guy was just happy I was okay—and so was I; it had been a scary situation. Life doesn't always go as you plan. I was lucky to be surrounded by good doctors and family, and my fifth grader was not scarred by me missing his ceremony. We are all human, and stuff happens; forgive yourself, be grateful, learn from the experience, and move on. Sometimes the most special days are the little events, so treasure them all and don't worry if you occasionally drop the ball, even on the big days!

Avoiding Social Media

We are all too addicted to our phones and devices; most disturbing is witnessing the way social media have burdened and created so much anxiety in our children, including mine.

I can't go back now, but if I were a young mom raising kids today, I would keep them away from smartphones, iPads, and all electronics for as many years as I possibly could. I would hold out longer than I did with mine, who didn't get phones until eighth grade.

The minute we give them access, we create a dangerous connection between that machine and their little brain.

I see so many kids in strollers with phones in their hands, and I want to reach out and tell their moms, "Don't do it! Give them a book or a toy! They are still so little." The addiction to artificial stimuli transpires so quickly, and they aren't yet ready to combat all that incoming.

By the time my kids were in high school, it was probably too late, but I still tried. I had them leave their phones at the back door in the mudroom when they walked into the house. I had them sit at the dining room table with their bags and their books and do their homework, as though they were in a study room. I think that knowing that my husband and I were always just a few steps away made them slightly less likely to scroll their devices or go online. I just wish I had done more, sooner.

There's no way to completely prevent kids from having access to all that is out there, but I think that putting up roadblocks, even if it's only for twenty minutes a day, is beneficial. A great place to start is at meals, particularly at a restaurant. Instead of letting a movie play on their device screen to keep them occupied, take advantage of that family time together. It's the perfect opportunity to not only bond with them through good old-fashioned conversation but teach them manners and help them learn that there's an appropriate time and place for everything.

Kids need guidance and rules. As the adults in the room, it's our responsibility to provide that for them. They may be mad in the moment, when we're laying down the law, but they will thank us for it later.

I firmly believe that.

CHAPTER 15

Jennifer Hegseth

Vice President of Programming, FOX Nation

"Don't 'should' all over yourself."

Anyone who knows Jennifer Hegseth will tell you that she is a superwoman in both her professional and personal lives. When I was introduced to Jen, she had a different last name and a different job, executive producer of *FOX & Friends*. At the time, I was already impressed by her work ethic, commitment, and conceptual understanding of morning television. Now not only does she still have a big job at FOX, but she married Pete Hegseth, a well-known *FOX &*

Friends Weekend host, and together they are raising seven beautiful children. Amazing!

As a working mom I can relate to Jen, but my respect for her as a strong, loving mother in a blended family is what makes her incredible in my eyes. Having a blended family myself, I know all too well the challenges it can bring and how often only time can overcome them. Her ability to take complex situations and make sense of them through practicality and commitment as she navigates it all is truly incredible.

Blended with Love

Marriage isn't always easy, but divorce never is. When I married my husband, Pete, we both had been married previously. We each brought three children into our home, and then we had a little girl together, making seven.

Divorce was something neither of us had dealt with during our childhood. Because we didn't have our own experience to draw from, we didn't know how to talk to our kids about certain things. So many questions and worries went through our minds: How do we explain divorce? Will a blended family work? Are our kids going to be okay? The biggest question we kept asking ourselves was, "What can we do for them?"

We realized that all we could do was pray, love them, and do *our* thing. That's the triad we found that works for our kids: show them unwavering love, show them how to love one another, and teach them to love and trust God.

What ended up being a blessing for us was that all of our children were young when we married. Our family, with all its various parts, just became what they knew. They are brothers and sisters, full stop. Kids are so adaptable; adults could learn from them.

At first Pete and I thought we'd approach parenting the way we remembered from childhood. As kids, we both had individual focuses from our siblings as far as getting involved in a ton of extracurricular sports and activities. As a child I didn't realize how hard it probably was for my parents to make my—and my sister's—world spin with scheduling, transportation, and everything else that goes along with it. As a mom, I now know.

With seven kids, we quickly realized that time constraints and custody schedules would impact our unrealistic pipe dream of each child being able to have their own busy schedule outside of school. So we decided to let go of the idolatry of sports and the idea that everyone was going to get to do everything separately, because unless we wanted a full staff of people raising our kids, it wasn't going to work. Each of them has activities, but family and church will always come first. Once we made that decision, we were free to maximize our family time.

That has become another magic ingredient for us; we try to do everything together. As a result, our children have a very special relationship with one another, and they know that family is top priority. Now they absolutely adore one another. They range in age from six to thirteen; they are alike and different in many ways. They're (mostly) graceful with one another, and there's enough of them that when one is annoyed with another, they can go hang out with someone else.

After living in New Jersey for several years as a family, we decided to move to Tennessee last year. The societal landscape had become so scary that we felt that sending them out the door was like sending them into a cultural ambush without any protection. We don't want them to be raised in a bubble, but like all parents, we want to protect and teach them until they can fend for themselves. Tennessee provided the right environment for us in the form of an amazing school, communities that are faith filled (towns have way more churches than Starbucks), and the freedom to raise your kids as *you* see fit and not as the government would like you to. Since the move, many people have asked me if the kids all now have their own rooms rather than sharing. The answer is no. They've always shared and will continue to do so. To be honest, they like sharing rooms, and it reinforces our goal of ensuring that they have strong bonds and love one another. It not only helps them bond, it teaches them to share, have patience, and work together. They also don't get to special order meals—everyone eats the same thing—because, as Pete says, "Communism is bad for governments but good for kids!"

It's easy for me to say, "Kids just need to know they are loved." It's harder to figure out how to do that, and I think a lot of moms struggle with *how* to love.

Boundaries, discipline, and expectations are an important part of loving your children, even when they don't like it. Sometimes men are better at this. I think a lot of moms struggle with wanting their kids to constantly be happy and feeling responsible for creating that happiness. We need to remember that kids find immediate and shallow happiness in silly things and it's our job to teach them and give them the feeling of real enjoyment and fulfillment. Sometimes that is hard to do.

One of our tougher rules is not allowing devices; no smartphones, iPads, smartwatches, internet-connected video games—nothing. To be honest, I was unsure how they (and I) would handle it since so many other kids have those gadgets. But they have just found other things to do: spending time together outside in the woods or in the creek, building a fort, playing board games, drawing, and my favorite: making up their own games! It is the same for our many family flights and road trips. It makes traveling much easier; nothing must be charged, and there are no gadgets to pack!

They still ask often why we have that rule and at what age it will change, but the peace of mind Pete and I have knowing that they can't easily access endless rabbit holes of information they're not ready for or forge relationships built on snaps and texts is so wonderful, I'm not sure if any of them will ever get a phone!

Moms need to remember this: kids have a very powerful way of making us rethink all our disciplinary decisions, both the big ones and the small ones, but you need to trust your mom self. You are the adult.

Setting Boundaries

As working moms, I think we are all asked frequently, "How do you balance it all?" Others may have different answers, but I can honestly say that there's no such thing as balance. It does not exist.

Once you accept that the key to survival with dueling work and home duties is *setting boundaries*, your life gets a lot better. It is way more important to me that my kids think I'm a good mom rather than a great career woman. So I look through that lens at every situation and choice I have to make. Being a great mom doesn't mean I have to go to every school event, sports game, or dance performance. If I can't be there, I make my presence felt with extra enthusiasm and encouragement beforehand or by sitting down with them afterward, one-on-one, to hear all the details.

The schedule is a constant roller coaster, and it's inevitable that someone is going to miss something (including lunches you forget to pack!)—and that's okay. You either constantly feel guilty about it or accept that it's the reality and make sure you put the priorities where *you* want them to be. Don't let the world's boundaries and expectations put them elsewhere for you.

Setting boundaries also means you have to focus and give 100 percent to what's in front of you at the time. So if there is such a thing as balance, it's temporary. Balancing means sometimes giving your attention to work and sometimes giving it to home, but when you try to do both at the same time, you'll feel anything but balanced. I can't be preoccupied with worrying about the kids, my house, or my husband and do my job well. I have to trust that whatever situation I have prepared for me to be able to work, whether it's a babysitter, day care, or school, will be fine.

When I had my first baby, that was an overwhelming concept. I looked at that little soul and thought, "How can I leave? Who will take care of him as well as his mom?" But then I realized that the people who care for our kids during the day aren't meant to replace us; they are there to keep them safe while we are away. But we are always their mom.

When I'm with the kids, I switch my focus to them. Their time with me is *their* time. I do everything I can to set that boundary and keep it. And at this point, they're old enough to remind me, "Mom, put the phone down!"

If I don't concentrate on one thing at a time, I'll constantly be pulled in every direction and always fall short at everything I do, with subpar results all around. I can't be the best mom, wife, and employee at all times, but I give my all to be the best I can when I am in each of these different roles.

Find Your Mom Community

Just as important as setting boundaries is learning to accept help. We have not only an unconventional family but an unconventional schedule. After some trial and error, Pete and I have figured out how to tag team to get everything done. I work from home Monday through Friday, and since my husband works weekends, he helps a lot with school pickups and drop-offs and the weekday stuff. On weekends, he jets off to New York City for work, so I'm solo, and I would be lying if I didn't admit that it can be tough at times. That was why I learned to accept help.

Take it from me, another essential tool for moms is to find your "mom community." Other mothers are going through the same thing you are, and some of them have more time during school hours, on the weekend, or just in general. Your mom community can help with some of the things that may seem monumental in the moment but really aren't, such as car pools and taking pictures of our kids when we can't be there. Other moms understand as nobody else can.

Working full-time and with so many kids, I find it nearly impossible to be everywhere for everything. It's okay—and very necessary—to recognize that you need help sometimes. So be sure to seek it out when you do. I think you'll find that people are usually very willing to lend a helping hand. A bonus is that the kids love it because it means they can spend more time with their friends. When I can't take them somewhere, my kids say, "Oh, I get to ride with so-and-so today!" It helps them build friendships. It's also good for them to learn early on that they, too, can lean on community and ask for help when they need it.

The RV

In the summertime, when everyone's on school break, there is one family ritual we especially love: our RV and camping road trips. Yes, to explore, but even more, to be together.

It might sound insane to travel with seven kids all piled together in one RV. And maybe it is, but it's the best kind of crazy. Even with ample space in the RV, the kids still find ways to sleep on top of one another instead of using all the other available spaces. It's actually one of my favorite ways we spend time together.

We don't allow electronic devices at home, so when we're on the road, the kids aren't complaining about missing them and can really get into the whole adventure. I believe they know how to socialize, interact, and think for themselves because they have to play with one another and are not distracted by devices.

After one of our earlier road trips, it's amazing that we continue the tradition because it certainly didn't go as planned.

Pete and I thought we were home free, renting a brand-spanking-new RV off the lot. She was shiny and beautiful, with only thirty-five miles on the odometer. We started in New Jersey and headed toward Minnesota, but along the way we stopped in various places, including the Ark Encounter in Williamstown, Kentucky, a jaw-dropping replica of Noah's Ark that is well worth the trip.

But it wasn't smooth sailing. The first hiccup happened as we were driving along in the middle of nowhere and we heard some kind of metal clanking and dragging behind the RV. When we looked in the rearview mirror, we saw something protruding from the undercarriage.

We wondered, "What is that? Is that supposed to happen?"

Pete pulled over to the side of the highway and got out to inspect the RV. Sure enough, the pipe sticking out that clearly shouldn't have been was for the generator. Without a functioning generator, we would lose all air-conditioning and other power.

So Pete grabbed some duct tape from inside the RV and lay on his back on the road with the traffic buzzing by to tape it up as best he could so we could keep going. We figured we could get it looked at at the next stop, but a few hours later there was another very scary moment: we lost the power steering and brakes as we were driving down the highway! Once Pete realized what had happened, he used all his muscle to keep the RV under control for more than an hour before we found a gas station.

We finally pulled into a rest area in northern Kentucky, Pete nearly hanging on the steering wheel to get it to turn. With a sigh of relief that we'd made it, we went inside to get help. However, there was no help to be had. The mechanics weren't on duty on Saturday. Our last hope was a card with the number of another local mechanic. With a lot of begging and explaining that we had seven kids in the RV, he finally agreed to come out with his tool kit and his teenage son. He found that a pipe for the power steering and brake fluid had burst, and he worked to replace it. Meanwhile, we played a board game at Denny's for the few hours it took to repair. Fun family time we weren't expecting, but the lemonade we made out of that lemon of a situation was supersweet. The kids all shook the mechanic's hand when he finished, and we hit the road toward the Brickyard 500 in Indianapolis.

As we pulled off the exit, with the Indianapolis Motor Speedway in our sights, it happened again! The steering and brakes completely failed, this time even worse. We pulled over and looked under the hood. Red fluid was spewing everywhere. We thought if we could just make it to the RV site, we'd be able to find some help. It is a car race, after all; there should be some mechanics around. So Pete muscled it a few miles through city traffic until we finally pulled into the site. We were relieved to make it in one piece; we set up camp and could already hear the cars buzzing by for the early races. We made a few calls to local mechanics and left numerous voicemails. While waiting for a return call, we watched the races with the kids, and rather than worrying and letting the broken RV ruin our day, we had a great time.

We assumed that people would get back to us even if it took a while on a weekend. We were wrong. Of the few who finally returned our call, the answer was "We can get this taken care of in about two weeks" or "Sorry, we don't work on RVs." By Monday morning, when the race was over and all the fans were gone, ours was the only RV left and we were still making calls. In our desperation we accidentally called the same place three times. The poor guy there had told us no every time, but he finally said, "You guys keep calling, I guess you really need help!"

"We really do!" we begged.

"Come on down, then," he replied.

So we muscled the RV to a corner garage in a tiny urban neighborhood. It did not look like an auto shop; it looked like a junkyard with a few junkyard dogs running around for good measure. But what looked unsettling ended up being our saving grace. That man could probably have taken the entire RV apart and put it back together before I could make dinner. He ran (literally) back and forth to the auto store several times, trying to make some sort of repair work. At one point, he said, "This is going to void your warranty, but it will get you where you need to go."

And we said, "Let's do it!"

I walked the kids in their matching Kyle Busch shirts down the highway to McDonald's; then they played with the dogs and watched what real work looks like while Pete and that man spent five hours trying to fix the issue. The man didn't have the right parts, but he created them out of what he did have. It was a great lesson in ingenuity and skilled labor for our kids to see.

Our angel mechanic finally patched the RV together enough to get us back on the road, and we eventually made it to Minnesota. Even though it was a disaster on one level, it never really felt like one; it felt like an adventure. We took each moment in stride and included the kids in the ups and downs. The truth was that we didn't really have anywhere to be because we were already where we wanted to be—with one another. It may have been a bit hectic at the time, but everything we do together becomes a wonderful memory.

Don't Sweat the Small Stuff

Part of how I handled that RV trip comes from lessons from my mom, Linda. My mother's parenting style was low drama. She was very reasonable, and I took my cues for how to react to things from her. As we all do, I open my mouth now and her words come out. I'd prefer that they didn't all come out ("Because I said so!"), but I want to focus on the ones that are really helpful.

Don't sweat the small stuff . . . it's all small stuff.

That was one of my favorites and is so important to keeping perspective.

Don't "should" all over yourself.

Should I have done this? Should I have said that? Just stop—because living in a constant state of questioning your decisions will get you nowhere fast.

She also had a piece of paper with the quote "Good morning! This is God. I have it all under control. I do not need your help." taped to the inside of the kitchen cabinet. It was the first thing she would read every morning when she reached for her coffee mug. I now have that same piece of paper in my kitchen.

I'm still discovering the seeds of wonderful things my parents planted inside me long ago, and I will never be able to thank them for all of it, but I can tell you, your kids will reap what you sow, whether you know it or not. I'll probably have to wait at least thirty years for our kids to appreciate the way we're raising them.

And that's okay.

CHAPTER 16

Sandra Smith

Coanchor, *America Reports*

"It's not the *quantity* of time you spend with them that matters most, it's the *quality*."

During the 2020 covid pandemic, Sandra Smith and I did near-daily interviews together on *America Reports*. It was early March, people were in a state of panic, and truth be told, so were we. Over the next few months, Sandra and I sent messages back and forth about what we were doing in various covid-related scenarios because, like most parents', our priority was how to keep our kids safe. We would worry together about how our kids were handling everything and laugh at ourselves for some of the things we were doing, such as wiping down packages and carrying hand sanitizer everywhere. Being able to laugh with her during such a difficult situation made the pandemic more bearable. She also had huge concerns about what the lockdowns were doing to the well-being of our children, something I was also very worried about. She is a great mom. She is a talented journalist as well, but her love for her children supersedes everything else.

In 2016, Sandra made history as half of one of the first dual-female teams to host a presidential primary debate—and she did it with two children under two years old at home.

Whether she's reporting on location from England for live coverage of Prince Harry's wedding to Meghan Markle, providing breaking news coverage of the Ukraine war, or hosting shows on FOX, she still faces the same question all moms face: Can I do it all?

The Same, but Different

I am the youngest of six children, the fifth daughter, and I have one brother. My mom is amazing; she always led the way for us. She is one of those moms who, even now, prioritizes her children almost too much. She is Oklahoma born and bred and has that wonderful southern midwest way about her. She always gave us unconditional love and support and was my biggest cheerleader. She still is. My mom is a big part of who I am as a working professional and also as a mother.

Mom stayed at home for the duration of all my siblings' upbringings. But I got to experience another side of her when she decided to go back to college later in life. I was in middle school and saw the independence she gained by earning an associate degree and entering the workforce. The change I witnessed in her was really special, and I think that also had a big part to play in who I am as a mother.

My mom instilled in me early on that family is everything. She impressed upon us that we should be supporting one another in everything and be there for your kids when they need you. That's part of who she is.

I could feel her influence on me from the moment I gave birth to my first baby, Cora. Motherhood didn't feel foreign; it felt familiar. Motherhood was instinctual and came naturally to me. I had an automatic connection to my baby and would do anything to protect her.

I'm very similar to my mom in that way; I prioritize my children almost too much. Sometimes I think I'm overcompensating for the working aspect of my life. Maybe that's not a bad thing, because I do work as much as I do and am away from home a lot. I know I'm not the only working parent to experience how hard it is to be away from our children. And so when you have time with them, it is everything. When I'm with my kids, I seize those moments and give them every piece of me.

As the sixth kid in the family, I was given a lot of free range, because I had a lot of free time, and too often that meant a lot of boredom. I didn't like that. I think that's why I'm exposing my kids to myriad interests: musical instruments, the arts, sports, and many other activities. Having them involved in activities keeps them busy, not bored.

Another departure from my upbringing is that my parents were of an era where you didn't speak openly with your children about a lot of things. I understand that it was a different time and norm, but my husband and I are way more open with our kids. I have always told my kids, "You can ask us about anything that's on your mind." As a result, they're very open with us. I like the fact that my daughter is willing to come to me and that she is not shy of doing so about anything that's going on in her life.

What We Don't Say Out Loud but Should

I worked straight through my pregnancies, then came back from maternity leave and dived right into covering serious events both times. That was true particularly when my son, Johnny, came into this world.

A few weeks after FOX launched *Outnumbered* in April 2014, I found out I was pregnant with my second child. I was excited to be having another child, whom I eventually learned was a boy. But the show was new, and I had committed to it, so I worked on *Outnumbered* right up until Johnny was born in January 2015.

Then my schedule got even more complicated. Even though I already had one new show on FOX, I was asked to anchor another one in a new lineup on FOX Business Network. But that one started at 5:00 a.m.

So I kicked off the 5:00 a.m. show, reported on others in between, then cohosted *Outnumbered* from noon to 1:00 p.m. every day. I had learned after Cora was born that life as a mom would take a certain amount of juggling, but that was an incredible amount to be doing every single moment of the day.

I was fortunate to have my amazing husband, John, in my corner. We made a decision together for him to back off from his work schedule a bit because things were getting crazy with all the pressures in mine. That way, he would be able to be with the kids more when I was unable to. We also found a great babysitter, and I'm also eternally grateful to my sister and niece, who pitched in as well. It really does take a village.

Shortly after Johnny was born, I somehow managed to host both those shows and thought there couldn't possibly be more room in my world to add another big responsibility. However, I was soon asked to comoderate the first of two presidential primary debates for FOX Business. One came up at the end of 2015 and one at the beginning of 2016. So we had to immediately start planning and prepping for the huge debate stages. It may look as though we are sitting and asking simple questions, but it takes a large amount of preparation. There is so much information to research, study, and digest on each individual candidate, let alone maneuver the live drama that happens on those stages with so many people vying for the most powerful job in the world once the cameras are on.

You're also on the ground with your team for a solid week for each debate. It was an amazing time to be a working mom, but it was a lot of pressure, and there were times I wasn't sure I could manage it all. Johnny was so tiny and I was still nursing, so everywhere we traveled the baby went with us, from Milwaukee, Wisconsin, to Charleston, South Carolina.

I think it's natural to wonder: Should I spend more time with my child? You see how hectic life can be, and you think, "Gosh, if I was just at home, we'd be so much more organized, we wouldn't be in a rush all the time." You aren't preoccupied in real time thinking about dropping your job, but you do wonder what life would have been like if you had stayed at home and given your kids all your time. I don't think most women say that out loud, but I think it's important for working moms to say it and share what they're thinking with other moms.

At the end of the day, I wouldn't change anything. I'm so proud of my kids, and as they get older, I think they're proud of me, too.

Let Some Things Go

In our household, keeping all of our schedules straight is one of the hardest tasks. There's the professional schedule, which has a lot of moving parts, as well as the children, who are older now at eight and ten and participating in a ton of activities. So we have to put everything into a daily calendar that we all reference. If it's not on the calendar, it doesn't happen.

I talk to moms about this all the time, and everyone has a fascinating answer to how to manage the schedules because we are all facing the same dilemma. Either they have a big, color-coded whiteboard in their kitchen, or they are old school and have a paper calendar. Some people, such as my husband, use the Google electronic calendar. I have a whiteboard *and* a paper desk calendar.

We are all asking the same questions: Can I have it all? Can I do it all?

The answer is *no.*

Even with all that planning, you have to come to terms with the fact that you can't be everywhere all the time. You have to let some things go. You really do have to make peace with it and make the most of the time you have with your kids instead of pushing for more time. It's not the *quantity* of time you spend with them that matters most, it's the *quality*. So when you miss something, don't be too hard on yourself. Believe me, I have not perfected any of this, and I still need to remind myself every day.

Just this morning, we woke up and realized that we had misread my second grader's school calendar and his biography project was actually due *today*, not next week as we had thought. I sent the teacher an email and she said he could turn it in another day. But it was awful when we drove up to school in the morning and dropped off my son and saw everybody holding their poster boards except for Johnny.

He's such a sweet and kind kid. He said, "Mom, it's okay." But sometimes I wonder. I don't know, and that's part of the worry.

I was beating myself up: What did I get wrong? I should have known. How could I send my son to school unprepared? The last thing I wanted was for him to feel bad because of something I had forgotten. I felt awful.

But all that stress isn't going to help anyone. So we have to forgive ourselves, let it go, and do better next time. My son will present his project tomorrow, and life *will* go on.

FINAL THOUGHTS

Being a mother is a profound and rewarding journey filled with countless moments of joy, struggle, and love. Mothers are blessed with experiencing the unique privilege of nurturing and guiding the growth of our children, and in doing so, we develop an appreciation for the small, everyday miracles of life.

I have been blessed with being surrounded by incredible women in every phase of motherhood—my family, friends, and colleagues, with some of whom I have been a part of their breast cancer diagnosis. Regardless of how they have come into my life, I have learned much from them, and it has been my honor to share some of their stories.

Gratitude as a mother is rooted in the bonds formed, the memories created, and the knowledge that one plays a vital role in shaping the future. It's an experience that teaches the art of selflessness and offers the gift of unconditional love. Motherhood can often be an overwhelming journey, filled with both joys and challenges. In those moments when the weight of the world feels too heavy, the support of family, friends, and God can make all the difference.

Whether it's a shoulder to lean on, a listening ear, or a helping hand, the love and assistance of your support network can provide solace, encouragement, and a renewed sense of resilience. It's a testament to the power of community and the bonds that hold us together, reinforcing the notion that in the world of motherhood, we are never truly alone.

xo, Nicole

ACKNOWLEDGMENTS

Undoubtedly, the best books are created when powerful experiences are shared with others. I feel blessed to be able to tell not only my own motherhood story but those of fifteen other incredible moms who are on unique journeys that have helped shape them into the women they are today. Without strong mothers, our society would falter; we remain indebted to them for creating well-rounded children who are loyal, grateful, faithful, and, more than anything else, kind.

I am thankful to my family, who continue to encourage me to pursue things I am passionate about. There is nothing more fulfilling than motherhood, so when the opportunity arose to write about it, I jumped on it.

Thank you to Suzanne Scott, CEO of FOX News, who had the vision of what this beautiful book would become. Also to Jason Klarman, president of FOX Nation and executive vice president of marketing at FOX News; Michael Tammero, former senior vice president of marketing and brand strategy; and Kimberly Capasso, vice president of brand strategy & marketing at FOX News, all of whom contributed by helping create the concept and overseeing the daily progress of the project.

At HarperCollins, thank you to the incomparable Lisa Sharkey, senior vice president of creative development, and associate editor Maddie Pillari, who have been invaluable throughout the process, influencing every aspect of the publication.

And to Ainsley Earhardt, Kayleigh McEnany, Martha Mac-Callum, Jennifer Hegseth, Jennifer Griffin, Janice Dean, Rachel

Campos-Duffy, Carley Shimkus, Sandra Smith, Alicia Hall, Annette Hill, Allison Deanda, Amy Brandt, and our two FOX viewer moms and their daughters, Marion Champlain and Sandra Champlain and Emily Barron Smith and Juliet Hardesty, for allowing me to tell their incredible stories.

It is the stories of others that encourage us to be better versions of ourselves. Let us all live our lives full of humility, gratitude, and love and never let go of our natural curiosity about what more can be done.

PHOTOGRAPHY CREDITS

Chapter 1   Monika De Meyer Photography
Chapter 2   Courtesy of Janice Dean
Chapter 3   Shine Sparkle Snap Photography by Lindsay Veech
Chapter 4   Pasha Belman
Chapter 5   Courtesy of Rachel Campos-Duffy
Chapter 6   Courtesy of Juliet Hardesty
Chapter 7   Rodrigo Varela
Chapter 8   Courtesy of Carley Shimkus
Chapter 9   Joan Diana Photography
Chapter 10   Courtesy of Sandra Champlain
Chapter 11   Lana Wong
Chapter 12   Courtesy of Annette Hill
Chapter 13   Courtesy of Alicia Hall
Chapter 14   Courtesy of Martha MacCallum
Chapter 15   Courtesy of Jennifer Hegseth
Chapter 16   Jill C Smith Photography

ABOUT THE AUTHOR

NICOLE SAPHIER, MD, is nationally known for being a FOX News Channel contributor since 2018, breaking down the latest medical, health policy, and opinion news across all platforms. She is also the best-selling author of *Make America Healthy Again: How Bad Behavior and Big Government Caused a Trillion-Dollar Crisis*; *Panic Attack: Playing Politics with Science in the Fight Against COVID-19*; and the children's book *That's What Family's For*.

Dr. Saphier works full-time as an associate professor in radiology at Memorial Sloan Kettering Cancer Center and Weill Cornell Medical College in the New York City area, where she lives with her husband and three sons.

Follow her on Twitter @NBSaphierMD and on Instagram @nicolesaphier_md.